Alan Bradley

Holistically
Energies in Motion

Original Title: Holistically: Energies in Motion
Copyright © 2024 by Luiz Antonio dos Santos
All rights reserved to Booklas.com

This book is intended for personal and spiritual development. The information and practices described are based on studies, traditional knowledge, and the experiences of authors and experts in the field. This content is not a substitute for medical advice or conventional therapies, serving as a complementary resource for well-being and personal growth.

Production Team

- **Editor**: Luiz Antonio dos Santos
- **Text Revision**: Evelyn Carter, James Williams, Olivia Bennett
- **Graphic Design and Layout**: Rachel Taylor
- **Cover Design**: Booklas Studio / Michael Brown

Publication and Identification
Holistically: Energies in Motion / By Leon Prado
Booklas, 2024
Categories: Personal Development. Spirituality. Religion.
I. Prado, Leon. II. Taylor, Rachel. III. Title.
DDC: 158.1 CDU: 159.9

All Rights Reserved
Booklas Publishing
José Delalíbera Street, 962
86.183-550 – Cambé – PR
Email: support@booklas.com
www.booklas.com

Sumary

Prologue 5
Chapter 1 The Veiled Origin... 7
Chapter 2 Fragmented Flows 11
Chapter 3 Lost Reconnection.. 15
Chapter 4 The Universal Archetype.. 19
Chapter 5 Cycles and Spirals 23
Chapter 6 Temporal Portals 27
Chapter 7 The Invisible Web 31
Chapter 8 Universal Vibration 35
Chapter 9 The Echoes of Creation 39
Chapter 10 Parallel Dimensions.. 43
Chapter 11 The Heart's Field.. 47
Chapter 12 The Paths of Water 51
Chapter 13 Ancestral Memories 55
Chapter 14 The Cosmic Mind... 60
Chapter 15 Light and Shadow... 65
Chapter 16 The Inner Labyrinth.. 69
Chapter 17 The Roots of the Earth.. 73
Chapter 18 Primal Sounds... 77
Chapter 19 Elemental Keys... 82
Chapter 20 Power Centers... 86
Chapter 21 Dance of the Forces.. 90
Chapter 22 The Cosmic Wheel 94
Chapter 23 Energy in Motion.. 98
Chapter 24 The Subtle Language 102

Chapter 25 Everyday Rituals 106
Chapter 26 Hidden Guardians 110
Chapter 27 Energetic Balance 115
Chapter 28 Cosmic Geometry 119
Chapter 29 Vital Breath 123
Chapter 30 Transformative Flames 127
Chapter 31 Silent Wisdom 131
Chapter 32 A Call to Unity 135
Chapter 33 The Shared Journey 139
Chapter 34 The Flow of Forgiveness 143
Chapter 35 Anchoring Light 147
Chapter 36 Lunar Reconnection 151
Chapter 37 Energetic Shields 155
Chapter 38 Transcendental Journey 159
Chapter 39 Voices of the Cosmos 163
Chapter 40 Seeds of Intention 167
Chapter 41 The Web of Life 171
Chapter 42 Residual Energy 175
Chapter 43 Inner Cycles 179
Chapter 44 A New Horizon 183
Chapter 45 Spiritual Pathways 187
Chapter 46 Conscious Prosperity 191
Chapter 47 Inner Flame 195
Chapter 48 Final Harmony 199
Chapter 49 Return to the Whole 203
Epilogue 207

Prologue

In the pages you are about to explore lies something profound, something that pulses beyond what the eyes can see and the tangible world can offer. This book is not merely a collection of words; it is a portal. Each line holds more than stories, concepts, or reflections. It is a personal invitation to uncover the unseen, a call for you to touch the forces that have always existed, waiting only for your awareness to awaken them.

Do you feel it? An energy flows around you, silent yet unceasing. It doesn't matter if you call it vitality, flow, or simply an unexplainable intuition. It is there—a timeless, insistent whisper that modern science has only just begun to decipher. Yet the truths contained here cannot be confined to theories or formulas. They vibrate at the core of what it means to be human, in what connects the individual to the cosmos.

Across the stories of ancient cultures and myths that have endured millennia, there is a haunting consensus: a primordial force exists, a current underlying all that lives and breathes. Different traditions have given it various names—qi, prana, mana. But names are mere symbols. What matters is the impact—tangible, transformative, absolute—of understanding and aligning with this universal flow.

This journey is not merely for the intellect. It calls upon what you feel, your ability to dive into the depths of yourself and perceive what has always been there, though perhaps ignored. You need not be an initiate in ancient rituals or an expert in quantum physics. All that is required is your willingness to open your eyes to a truth that resides both within and outside you, echoing in every gust of wind, in every beat of your heart.

You were drawn here for a reason. Perhaps it is the desire to understand the inexplicable or to find answers to questions that have lingered in your mind. Perhaps it is something deeper—an instinct, an intuition—that has brought you here. But know this: what lies ahead goes far beyond what you might expect.

Allow yourself to consider the impact of reconnecting with this primordial force. Imagine how it would feel to find meaning in the seemingly random patterns of life, to see clarity where there was once chaos. This book will not give you all the answers, but it will equip you with the tools to ask the right questions—the ones that resonate with the deepest part of your being.

You are about to explore the invisible web that connects all things. The stories and teachings you will find are not merely relics of the past; they are invitations for the present and the future. They serve as a reminder that you are not merely a passive observer in this world. You are an active part, connected by invisible threads to all beings, to all creation.

Each page is a step forward on a path many have walked, yet it remains unique for every traveler. The discoveries you make will not merely expand your knowledge—they will shape you, transforming not only what you know but who you are.

So, read carefully. Feel the words deeply. What lies ahead is not an end, but a beginning—a portal to what has always been within your reach, waiting to be seen.

Chapter 1
The Veiled Origin

Beneath the folds of history lies a force as old as creation itself. It has been whispered by sages, drawn by the trembling hands of ancient artists, and felt by those attuned to the quiet hum of the universe. Known by many names—*qi, prana, mana,* or simply "life force"—this emanation transcends culture, language, and time. To trace its origin is to peer through a veil obscured by millennia of reverence and mystery.

In the cradle of humanity, the earliest ancestors sought to understand the forces that animated their world. The hunt, the harvest, the birth of a child—each was seen as more than a physical act but as a dance with unseen energies. They observed how the wind carried whispers through the trees and how water, with its unfathomable depths, seemed to pulse with a rhythm all its own. This silent dialogue with nature shaped the foundation of what we now call vital energy.

Evidence of these early explorations is etched into stone and earth. In the caves of Chauvet, France, the flickering torchlight reveals images of animals mid-stride, their forms vibrating with a lifelike energy. These were no mere depictions but invocations, attempts to capture the essence, the emanation that imbued all living things. Across the ocean, in the Australian Outback, Aboriginal Dreamtime stories speak of an ancestral energy flowing through songlines, connecting the land, people, and stars.

From the plains of Mesopotamia to the peaks of the Himalayas, myths emerged to describe this enigmatic force. In India, the Upanishads spoke of *prana*, the breath of life that sustains all beings. Chinese sages, observing the cycles of nature, described *qi*, a universal energy flowing through the heavens and earth. The Greeks, too, had their *pneuma*, a vital spirit believed to animate the cosmos.

Each culture, in its own way, sought to articulate this invisible truth. While their languages and symbols varied, the essence of their understanding remained remarkably similar. They all recognized that life was more than matter—it was movement, vibration, and connection.

As the human mind evolved, so too did methods for working with these energies. In ancient Egypt, priests engaged in rituals to channel the life force through sacred geometry and resonant chants. Temples were constructed not merely as places of worship but as conduits for these energies, aligning with celestial patterns to amplify their power. Similarly, in pre-Columbian America, the shamans of the Andes used *qhapac nan*, or the "Great Energy Path," to draw power from the mountains and stars.

Anthropological records reveal a profound respect for these forces, preserved in oral traditions and sacred practices. In Polynesia, navigators guided their canoes across vast oceans using an intuitive connection with the energy of the waves and stars. The Dogon people of West Africa, with their intricate knowledge of Sirius, spoke of a life force descending from the heavens to shape humanity.

Yet, this reverence for emanations was not confined to spirituality. It intertwined seamlessly with daily life. Healers became adept at sensing and manipulating these energies to restore balance and vitality. Farmers planted their crops in harmony with cosmic rhythms, believing that the unseen energies of the heavens affected the fertility of their soil.

Even as civilizations rose and fell, the wisdom of these emanations endured, passed down like a sacred thread woven into the fabric of humanity. It was both a science and an art, demanding attunement, observation, and humility.

The veil, however, was never fully lifted. The origins of this force remain shrouded in mystery, even as modern science begins to probe its edges. Archaeologists uncover artifacts suggesting advanced knowledge of energetic principles—amulets designed to channel protective forces, structures aligned with magnetic ley lines, and relics resonating with frequencies tuned to the earth's vibrations.

In these discoveries lies a question as ancient as the force itself: where did it come from? Some say it was born in the cosmic explosion that seeded the universe, a ripple of energy echoing through eternity. Others see it as the breath of a divine creator, an essence imbued with purpose and meaning.

The Veiled Origin reminds us that understanding emanations is not a matter of solving a puzzle but of embracing a mystery. It is not a destination but a journey—a labyrinth where every turn reveals new layers of wonder and complexity.

Through comparative mythology, we find common threads that bind humanity's understanding of this force. The Norse *lifthrasir* speaks of a life-animating essence that will survive the end of the world, akin to the Hindu belief in the cyclical renewal of *prana*. In the myths of the Zuni, we encounter the *life breath* as a sacred trust, given to humanity by the gods and returned in death to the eternal flow.

This universality suggests something profound: that emanations are not a cultural artifact but a shared reality. They are as integral to existence as the air we breathe and the light that warms our skin. The ancient knowledge of these forces, though fragmented and obscured by time, still pulses beneath the surface of our modern world.

In rediscovering these truths, we are not merely looking back but also forward. The study of emanations offers a bridge between the ancient and the contemporary, the mystical and the scientific. It invites us to see the world not as a collection of isolated phenomena but as an interconnected web of energy, each thread vibrating with life and purpose.

The journey into the Veiled Origin is not one of answers but of revelations. It beckons us to listen—to the winds, the waters, and the silent hum of existence itself. Through this listening, we may begin to perceive the echoes of that primordial force, still flowing, still shaping, still alive within us all.

Chapter 2
Fragmented Flows

The river of understanding flows through every culture, yet its course diverges and splits, creating tributaries of interpretation. These fragmented flows are the myriad ways humanity has sought to categorize and work with the elusive energies that pulse through existence. Each tradition, born of its unique landscape, history, and perception, has charted its own map of the unseen. Together, they form a kaleidoscope of insight into the nature of emanations.

In the Eastern world, systems of energy are both intricate and profound. The meridians of Traditional Chinese Medicine (TCM) serve as pathways for *qi*, the life force said to flow through every living being. These meridians interconnect in a web-like structure, guiding energy to organs and tissues. Blockages in these pathways disrupt harmony, leading to disease—a concept that birthed practices like acupuncture, moxibustion, and *qigong*.

Across the Indian subcontinent, the Vedic tradition conceptualizes a similar network, though expressed through the *nadis*. These channels, numbering in the thousands, carry *prana* throughout the body, intersecting at energy centers called chakras. The ancient texts describe the three principal nadis—Ida, Pingala, and Sushumna—as conduits for spiritual awakening, their alignment unlocking higher states of consciousness.

Moving westward, the Jewish Kabbalah offers another lens through which to view these flows. The Sefirot, the ten emanations of the Tree of Life, represent the dynamic interplay of divine energy as it manifests in the world. Unlike the physical pathways of the East, these are spiritual dimensions, pathways of consciousness that bridge the infinite and the finite. Mystics who meditate upon the Sefirot seek not only understanding but transformation, aligning their inner being with the divine architecture of existence.

Shamanic traditions, spread across continents, add yet another perspective. In the Americas, practitioners have long worked with telluric currents—energies that rise from the earth and infuse the land. These currents are intimately connected with the spirits of place, natural forces that guide and protect communities. Shamans use rituals, dances, and sacred objects to attune to these flows, drawing upon them for healing and wisdom.

Despite their differences, these systems share striking parallels. Each describes a kind of "energetic cartography," a map that guides the practitioner through the unseen dimensions of reality. The symbols vary, yet the patterns they describe resonate with uncanny similarity. Energy flows in lines, spirals, and currents, moving within the individual and connecting them to the cosmos.

To understand the fragmented flows, one must look beyond the surface distinctions and examine the underlying principles. In TCM, the five elements—Wood, Fire, Earth, Metal, and Water—govern the movement of *qi*. These elements correspond to seasons, emotions, and organs, reflecting the interconnectedness of all things. The Indian concept of the *pancha mahabhutas* (Earth, Water, Fire, Air, and Ether) similarly describes the fundamental forces shaping both the macrocosm and microcosm.

Such systems offer not only metaphors but practical applications. In both TCM and Ayurveda, energy imbalances are diagnosed and treated through a variety of techniques, from herbal remedies to dietary adjustments. These practices are not merely therapeutic; they are deeply spiritual, rooted in the belief that harmony within reflects harmony without.

The fractured nature of these traditions often masks their shared origins. Scholars speculate that many energy systems may have evolved from common ancestral knowledge, disseminated through trade routes, migration, and cultural exchange. The Silk Road, for instance, was more than a network for goods—it was a highway for ideas. Along its paths, Indian *prana* may have influenced Chinese *qi*, while Greek *pneuma* blended with Egyptian and Mesopotamian concepts of life force.

But these flows were also shaped by isolation, molded to the unique needs and environments of their people. The Sefirot reflect the Kabbalistic focus on divine mystery, a legacy of the Jewish diaspora and its emphasis on preserving spiritual identity. Shamanic traditions, by contrast, evolved in closer harmony with nature, emphasizing direct communion with the spirits of the earth and sky.

The fragmentation, then, is not a flaw but a feature—a testament to humanity's boundless creativity in interpreting the ineffable. Each tradition illuminates a facet of the whole, a fragment of a universal truth too vast to be contained by any single system.

Yet, the question arises: how can we reconcile these diverse perspectives? Modern scholars and practitioners have attempted to weave these threads together, creating frameworks that honor their distinctiveness while exploring their unity. Comparative studies reveal how TCM meridians align with Vedic nadis, how the chakras correspond to the Sefirot, and how shamanic rituals echo the practices of both.

This synthesis is not without its challenges. Misunderstandings and oversimplifications abound, often diluting the depth of these traditions. True integration demands respect and rigorous study, an acknowledgment that the fragmented flows are not merely systems but living traditions, rooted in communities and cultures.

For those who seek to engage with these energies, the fragmented flows offer both a challenge and an opportunity. They invite exploration, not as a consumer of wisdom but as a participant in its unfolding. To walk the paths of the meridians, the nadis, or the Sefirot is to embark on a journey of transformation, guided by the maps of those who have walked before.

The fragmented flows remind us that the unseen is not separate from the seen but interwoven with it. They teach that energy is not confined to the body or the spirit but moves through all things, a constant exchange between the inner and outer worlds.

In these currents, one can find healing and harmony, not only for oneself but for the wider web of life. The meridians of TCM are mirrored in the rivers of the earth, the chakras in the vortexes of the land, the Sefirot in the cosmic patterns that shape galaxies. To understand them is to understand our place within the greater whole.

Though fragmented, these flows converge in a deeper truth: that all energy is one, moving in endless cycles of creation and transformation. The maps may differ, but the territory they describe is the same—a vast, interconnected web of emanations, vibrant with life and possibility.

To step into this web is to awaken to its presence, to feel the pulse of the unseen as it moves through and around us. It is to recognize that the fragmented flows are not fragments at all but the many faces of a singular, boundless force.

Chapter 3
Lost Reconnection

The thread that once bound humanity to the currents of subtle energy has frayed, a severance wrought not in a moment but over centuries of transformation. Beneath the march of progress lies a quieter story, one of disconnection from the emanations that once infused every facet of existence. To explore this loss is to uncover how the interplay of technology, philosophy, and culture has veiled humanity's intuitive sensitivity to these unseen forces.

The dawn of the Industrial Revolution marked the first rupture. As steam engines roared to life and factories cast their shadows over pastoral landscapes, a profound shift occurred. The rhythms of nature, once the heartbeat of daily life, were subsumed by the mechanical cadence of machines. Fields of crops gave way to steel, and the cycles of the moon yielded to the schedules of industry. Humanity's gaze, once turned toward the heavens and the earth, now looked inward, to the forges of its own creation.

With this shift came the rise of materialism. The world was reimagined as a machine, each part separate and distinct, governed by immutable laws. Subtle energies, once revered as the animating force of life, were dismissed as relics of superstition. The sacred became symbolic, and the unseen world was banished to the fringes of thought.

Yet, the disconnection was not immediate. Echoes of the old ways persisted in rural villages, where farmers planted by the lunar calendar and healers whispered prayers over the sick. In these pockets, the ancient knowledge lingered, a quiet resistance to the tide of progress.

By the 20th century, however, the disconnection had deepened. Urbanization pulled humanity further from the natural world, encasing millions in concrete jungles where the sky was often obscured by towering structures and smog. The once-intimate relationship with the earth became a distant memory, replaced by a dependency on artificial environments.

Modern lifestyles exacerbated the estrangement. The hum of electromagnetic fields, the glare of artificial lights, and the constant buzz of technology created an invisible barrier to the subtle vibrations of the natural world. Studies reveal how these influences dull the human capacity to perceive emanations, disrupting circadian rhythms and numbing intuitive faculties.

Electromagnetic pollution, a byproduct of the digital age, compounds the issue. Wireless networks, satellites, and electrical grids saturate the airwaves, creating a cacophony of artificial frequencies that interfere with the body's natural energy fields. Sensitives—those attuned to the unseen—speak of an energetic fog that clouds perception, a phenomenon increasingly recognized in studies of environmental sensitivity.

Yet, even in the midst of this disconnection, the yearning for reconnection persists. Practitioners of ancient traditions—yogis, shamans, and mystics—offer insights into the impacts of this loss. They describe a diminished ability to access intuitive states, a spiritual hunger that manifests as restlessness, anxiety, and a pervasive sense of emptiness.

This yearning has driven many to rediscover the old paths, seeking practical ways to bridge the divide. Simple practices, like grounding—walking barefoot on the earth—restore the body's connection to terrestrial energies. Meditation and breathwork, too, quiet the noise of modern life, allowing the subtle currents to be felt once more.

Scientific research supports these practices. Studies on the Schumann resonance, the natural electromagnetic frequency of the earth, reveal its profound effects on human physiology. When individuals are exposed to these frequencies, their brain waves align, fostering relaxation and heightened awareness. The science, though nascent, suggests that the ancient wisdom of connecting with the earth was not merely symbolic but deeply practical.

Urban centers, paradoxically, have become incubators for a renewed interest in these connections. Yoga studios, meditation centers, and holistic health practices proliferate, offering modern adaptations of ancient techniques. These spaces serve as sanctuaries, where individuals can momentarily escape the dissonance of contemporary life and touch something timeless.

The disconnection also spurred innovations in technology aimed at reconnection. Devices designed to shield against electromagnetic interference, sound therapy tools, and biofeedback systems reflect a growing recognition of the subtle energies influencing well-being. These modern approaches echo ancient practices, blending old knowledge with new methodologies.

Despite these efforts, the path to reconnection is fraught with challenges. The momentum of modernity often resists the introspection required to perceive emanations. Instant gratification, a hallmark of the digital age, clashes with the patience and discipline demanded by ancient practices.

Yet, the voices of those who have embarked on this path resonate with hope. Elders from indigenous communities recount the resurgence of sacred ceremonies, where the energies of the earth, sky, and spirit are invoked and honored. Practitioners of meditation describe moments of profound clarity, where the hum of existence becomes palpable. Researchers document the measurable changes in brain activity during states of deep connection, affirming what mystics have long known: that the unseen is not absent but simply overlooked.

To begin restoring this lost bond requires not a rejection of progress but a rebalancing. The tools of modernity can coexist with the wisdom of the past, each enhancing the other. A smartphone, for example, can guide one to a remote forest, where the subtle emanations of nature can be experienced firsthand.

The journey back to connection is deeply personal yet inherently collective. As individuals reclaim their sensitivity to emanations, the ripple effect touches families, communities, and ultimately, the world. Healing the disconnection within fosters harmony without, reminding humanity of its integral place within the web of life.

The disconnection from emanations is not a closed chapter but a turning point. It invites a deeper inquiry into how we live and relate to the unseen forces that sustain us. The loss, though profound, is not irreparable. The energies remain, flowing quietly beneath the surface, waiting to be felt, honored, and embraced once more.

Reconnection, then, is not merely a return but a renewal. It is the weaving of ancient threads into the fabric of the present, creating a tapestry that honors the past while envisioning the future. In this weaving lies the promise of rediscovering the currents that flow through all things, guiding humanity back to the heart of existence itself.

Chapter 4
The Universal Archetype

Hidden in the folds of collective memory lies a profound truth: humanity, scattered across the expanse of time and geography, has always returned to the same symbols, the same patterns, the same archetypes. These universal images are more than mere figments of imagination; they are bridges to a deeper reality, a connection to the emanations that pulse through existence. To uncover their meaning is to step into the timeless dance of the cosmos, where symbols, energies, and consciousness entwine in a sacred symphony.

The archetype is not born of culture but resonates through it, an eternal melody that shapes myths, art, and rituals. From the great Tree of Life that appears in the sacred texts of the Norse, Mayan, and Hebrew traditions to the serpent that coils in myths from ancient India to Mesoamerica, these images emerge not as isolated creations but as manifestations of something shared and universal. They are the language of the unseen, speaking to a part of the human spirit that exists beyond words.

Jungian psychology reveals the archetype as an imprint on the collective unconscious, a reservoir of inherited memories and symbols. Yet, Jung did not invent these ideas—he illuminated them, drawing upon traditions as ancient as humanity itself. These archetypes serve as conduits, connecting the individual psyche to the boundless web of emanations that permeate existence.

The Tree of Life, for instance, is not merely a symbol but an energetic axis connecting heaven, earth, and the underworld. In Norse mythology, Yggdrasil stands as the cosmic tree, its roots and branches linking the nine realms. The Kabbalistic Tree of

Life serves a similar purpose, mapping the flow of divine emanations through the Sefirot, guiding seekers toward spiritual enlightenment. These parallels suggest that the tree is more than metaphor—it is an archetype embedded in the fabric of reality, a reflection of the interconnected flows of energy within the cosmos.

Consider the sacred circle, an image that appears in countless traditions. The mandalas of Tibetan Buddhism, the medicine wheels of Native American spirituality, and the stone circles of Neolithic Europe all evoke the same archetypal energy: wholeness, balance, and eternity. The circle, with its unbroken form, mirrors the cycles of nature—the orbit of celestial bodies, the turning of seasons, the rhythms of birth, death, and renewal. To step into a sacred circle is to align oneself with these cycles, to become part of the greater flow of existence.

The serpent, too, winds its way through the collective consciousness, embodying both creation and destruction. In Hindu tradition, Kundalini is the coiled serpent energy that lies dormant at the base of the spine, waiting to rise and awaken higher states of consciousness. The Mesoamerican deity Quetzalcoatl, the feathered serpent, represents the union of earth and sky, the material and the divine. Across the globe, the serpent speaks of transformation, a reminder that energy, like life itself, is in constant motion.

These archetypes are not static—they are alive, shifting and adapting as they flow through cultures and eras. Their recurrence is not coincidence but resonance, a reflection of the fundamental energies that shape existence. They appear in dreams and visions, rituals and prayers, carrying messages from the unseen to the seen.

The connection between archetypes and emanations becomes even more apparent in sacred art and rituals. In the intricate carvings of ancient temples, the mandalas painted with meticulous precision, and the chants that echo through sacred spaces, archetypes are given form and voice. These creations are not merely aesthetic—they are tools for channeling and working with the subtle energies that flow through the universe.

Rituals, too, are acts of archetypal expression. The lighting of a candle, the drawing of a circle, the telling of a myth—each is a reenactment of an archetypal story, a way of aligning oneself with the universal forces represented by these symbols. The flame becomes the eternal light, the circle the cosmos, the myth a map of the soul's journey through the labyrinth of existence.

The archetypes also serve as guides for personal transformation. Within each person lies a pantheon of symbols, a reflection of the greater archetypal realm. The hero's journey, so often told in myths and stories, mirrors the individual's path of growth and self-discovery. The shadow, an archetype representing the unseen and rejected aspects of the self, challenges one to confront and integrate these hidden parts. The wise old man or woman, the nurturer, the trickster—each archetype appears in the psyche, offering lessons and insights into the flows of energy within and without.

In recognizing these archetypes, one begins to see their presence everywhere. The spiral of a galaxy mirrors the spiral of the Kundalini's rise. The ebb and flow of the tide reflect the dualities of light and shadow, creation and destruction. The archetypes reveal that the microcosm is a reflection of the macrocosm, that the individual is a fractal of the universe.

The study of these symbols also offers practical tools for spiritual development. By meditating on an archetype—be it the tree, the serpent, or the circle—one can attune to the energies it represents. Visualization exercises, in which one enters the sacred space of an archetype, foster a deep connection to its essence. Rituals that evoke archetypal symbols create a resonance between the practitioner and the greater flows of energy they embody.

Moreover, these archetypes remind humanity of its shared heritage. Despite the fragmentation of cultures and languages, the recurrence of these symbols speaks to a unity beneath the surface. They are a testament to the interconnectedness of all beings, a reminder that the flows of energy within one person are part of a greater current that moves through all life.

In the archetypes lies a profound truth: the emanations that shape the cosmos also shape the human spirit. To engage with these symbols is to enter into a dialogue with the universe, to hear its whispers and feel its currents. The archetypes are not relics of the past but living presences, guiding humanity toward a deeper understanding of itself and its place within the web of existence.

The Universal Archetype reveals that the language of symbols is the language of energy, a way of seeing the unseen and knowing the unknowable. It calls upon humanity to remember, to reconnect, and to honor the archetypes as gateways to the infinite. In doing so, one begins to perceive the intricate dance of emanations, where every symbol is a note, every archetype a chord, in the symphony of creation.

Chapter 5
Cycles and Spirals

Within the pulse of existence lies a pattern both ancient and unyielding. It manifests in the rise and fall of tides, the waxing and waning of the moon, the turning of seasons, and the rhythmic beat of a heart. Cycles define life, spirals carry it forward, and together they form the unseen pathways of emanations. These sacred patterns transcend mere observation; they reveal the nature of existence itself—dynamic, interconnected, and ever in motion.

From the smallest cell to the vast expanse of galaxies, spirals and cycles emerge as universal truths. The double helix of DNA, the fractal branches of a tree, and the spiral arms of the Milky Way each mirror the other. These forms are not coincidental; they are expressions of the underlying flows of energy that shape reality. To understand cycles and spirals is to glimpse the architecture of the universe and the currents of energy that move within it.

Among the earliest humans, awareness of these patterns was essential for survival. The cycles of day and night dictated activity, while the changing seasons determined the rhythms of planting and harvest. Ancient cultures developed sacred calendars, aligning their lives with cosmic cycles to harmonize with the unseen forces of nature. The Mayan Long Count calendar, the Vedic concept of *yugas*, and the lunar cycles observed in Chinese and Islamic traditions are not merely measures of time but reflections of energetic rhythms.

The spiral, as a symbol, transcends physical form. It represents the expansion and contraction of energy, the flow between creation and dissolution. Across cultures, it has been revered as a bridge between worlds. The Maori koru spiral signifies new life and growth, while the spiral petroglyphs of the Ancestral Puebloans are thought to mark points of energetic significance. In Celtic art, the triple spiral—*triskelion*—echoes the cycles of birth, death, and rebirth.

At the heart of these patterns lies the interplay of opposites: light and shadow, growth and decay, ascent and descent. These dualities are not conflicts but complements, their tension giving rise to motion. In Taoist philosophy, the *yin* and *yang* symbolize this balance, their dynamic interplay forming the rhythm of existence.

Biorhythms, the cycles governing living beings, further illustrate these flows. The circadian rhythm, for instance, governs sleep and wakefulness, aligning with the sun's journey across the sky. The lunar cycle influences not only tides but also human emotions and behaviors, its phases subtly altering the flows of energy within. Studies on women's menstrual cycles reveal an intrinsic connection to the moon, an echo of ancient wisdom that modern science is only beginning to grasp.

The celestial bodies also play a role in shaping these spirals and cycles. Solar and lunar eclipses, solstices, and equinoxes act as energetic gateways, amplifying the currents that flow through the cosmos. The Great Year, or precession of the equinoxes, unfolds over millennia, reflecting humanity's journey through epochs of spiritual evolution. These vast cycles remind us that time is not linear but cyclical, a spiral in which each revolution brings new perspectives and possibilities.

Energetic traditions have long worked with these patterns to enhance harmony and vitality. In Chinese medicine, the five elements correspond to the seasons and the cycles of nature. Practitioners use this understanding to align their treatments with the patient's unique energetic rhythm. Similarly, the Vedic tradition's *panchanga* (astrological calendar) guides rituals and practices to synchronize with cosmic flows.

Practical techniques for aligning with cycles and spirals abound. Meditation during the full moon amplifies clarity and intuition, while rituals at the new moon foster introspection and renewal. Seasonal ceremonies, such as solstice celebrations, honor the transitions of light and shadow, aligning participants with the greater cycles of the earth.

Modern research affirms the significance of these rhythms. Studies on circadian biology reveal the profound impact of light cycles on human health, influencing everything from mood to metabolism. Disruptions to these rhythms, such as those caused by artificial lighting or erratic schedules, can lead to dissonance in body and mind, a modern echo of humanity's estrangement from natural flows.

At a broader level, cycles govern collective energies as well. Societies rise and fall in rhythms, their golden ages and declines echoing cosmic patterns. The ancient Hindu concept of *yugas* describes these cycles of civilization, from the spiritually enlightened *Satya Yuga* to the materialistic and chaotic *Kali Yuga*. Whether viewed through mythological or sociological lenses, these patterns suggest that humanity's journey is not random but guided by larger forces.

The spiral is not merely a symbol of cycles; it is a pathway of evolution. While cycles may repeat, the spiral adds a dimension of progress, carrying energy forward through growth and transformation. It reflects the soul's journey, where each return to a familiar point offers a chance to ascend, to see from a higher perspective.

Sacred geometry captures these truths in form. The Fibonacci sequence, the golden ratio, and other mathematical patterns found in nature reveal the spiral as a blueprint for creation. The nautilus shell, the arrangement of sunflower seeds, and the galaxies above all follow these principles, affirming that the spiral is a universal expression of life's emanations.

Working with spirals involves more than observation—it is an act of participation. Practices like labyrinth walking allow one to physically engage with the spiral, mirroring the inward and outward flows of energy. These meditative journeys align the practitioner with the rhythms of existence, fostering balance and insight.

The cycles and spirals also serve as reminders of impermanence. Nothing remains static; everything flows, changes, and returns. This awareness invites not despair but reverence, a recognition that life's beauty lies in its motion. By embracing these patterns, one learns to move with the currents rather than resist them, finding harmony within the inevitable ebb and flow.

To live in alignment with cycles and spirals is to become attuned to the rhythms of the universe. It is to recognize that each breath, each heartbeat, each revolution of the earth is part of a greater dance. The cycles guide us, the spirals elevate us, and together they reveal the sacred flows of energy that connect all things.

Through this understanding, the fragmented becomes whole, the transient eternal. The cycles and spirals remind us that life, in all its complexity, is not a straight line but a continuous journey of return and renewal. They call us to step into the rhythm, to feel the currents, and to dance with the emanations that shape the cosmos and our place within it.

Chapter 6
Temporal Portals

Time is not merely a linear procession but a fabric woven with moments of heightened significance, where the ordinary dissolves and the extraordinary emerges. These are the temporal portals—specific junctures where the flows of emanations intensify, altering perception, opening pathways, and amplifying energies. They are the hinges upon which the doorways of transformation swing, inviting those who step through to engage with the unseen currents of existence.

The recognition of these temporal gateways stretches back to the earliest whispers of human consciousness. Ancient cultures attuned to the rhythms of the cosmos identified specific times when energy flowed with unique intensity. These moments, often aligned with celestial phenomena, were revered as opportunities for insight, renewal, and transcendence. The solstices, equinoxes, and planetary alignments became sacred markers, their significance echoed in myths, rituals, and monumental constructions.

The solstices stand as some of the most profound examples of temporal portals. At the winter solstice, the longest night gives way to the gradual return of light, symbolizing rebirth and renewal. For ancient cultures, this was a time of celebration and deep reflection, marked by rituals that called forth the sun's return. Stonehenge, aligned perfectly with the solstitial sun, reveals the precision with which our ancestors honored this temporal gateway.

Equinoxes, where day and night achieve perfect balance, hold their own energetic significance. They represent equilibrium, a moment to harmonize opposing forces within and without. Across the globe, cultures celebrated these thresholds—spring equinox for fertility and new beginnings, autumn equinox for harvest and gratitude. These times, where balance prevails, offer a fleeting window to align oneself with the cosmos.

Beyond the seasonal markers, planetary alignments and lunar cycles have also been revered as temporal portals. The full moon, with its luminous presence, has long been associated with heightened intuition and emotional energy. Rituals performed under its light draw upon its amplifying power, channeling energies toward manifestation or release. Similarly, eclipses—moments of cosmic shadow and light—have been viewed as times of profound transformation, where the veil between worlds thins.

Historical accounts reveal the impact of these temporal portals not just on individuals but on entire civilizations. The Aztecs, for instance, meticulously tracked Venus's cycles, aligning rituals and decisions with its movements. The ancient Egyptians synchronized key events with Sirius's heliacal rising, a celestial event that marked the flooding of the Nile and the renewal of life. These civilizations understood that the flows of time were not uniform but punctuated by moments of extraordinary potency.

Temporal portals are not limited to grand celestial events. They also manifest in personal and collective experiences. Moments of profound synchronicity, where coincidence feels infused with meaning, act as individual temporal gateways. On a larger scale, historical periods of upheaval or inspiration often coincide with energetic shifts—revolutions, renaissances, and revelations arising as collective energies reach a crescendo.

Modern science, though often skeptical of ancient interpretations, is beginning to explore the energetic significance of time. Studies on biorhythms and circadian biology reveal how certain times of day optimize physical and mental states, aligning with natural cycles of energy. Research into solar flares and geomagnetic activity uncovers correlations between these cosmic events and human behavior, suggesting a subtle but profound link between the heavens and the mind.

For those who seek to engage with temporal portals, practices abound. Meditation timed with significant celestial events fosters alignment with the amplified flows of energy. Rituals, whether simple or elaborate, transform these moments into sacred acts, channeling intention through the portal's opening. Techniques such as journaling during solstices or equinoxes capture the insights and shifts that arise, anchoring them into conscious awareness.

Temporal portals are not passive—they are catalysts. They amplify intention, accelerate transformation, and deepen connection to the unseen currents. For this reason, preparation is essential. Entering a temporal gateway without clarity can amplify confusion or imbalance. Thus, grounding practices, setting intentions, and cultivating presence become vital tools for navigating these moments.

Beyond harnessing existing portals, it is possible to create personal temporal gateways. Practices such as fasting, breathwork, and meditation alter perception, intensifying one's connection to subtle energies. Ceremonies that mark transitions—birthdays, anniversaries, or milestones—imbue ordinary moments with sacred significance, transforming them into portals of intentional change.

Temporal portals also invite a reflection on the nature of time itself. Modernity often reduces time to a commodity, measured and parceled into schedules and deadlines. Yet, the existence of these gateways reveals a deeper truth: time is not merely chronological but qualitative. It ebbs and flows, its currents shaped by the interplay of cosmic and earthly forces.

In acknowledging this truth, one begins to see time not as a linear constraint but as a living, dynamic force. The spiral patterns of history, the rhythms of nature, and the cycles of the cosmos all point to time as a carrier of emanations, its portals opening and closing like breaths in the great lung of existence.

Through these portals, humanity is reminded of its place within the vast web of creation. The solstices and equinoxes ground us in the turning of the earth; the eclipses and alignments connect us to the heavens; the personal milestones anchor us in the unfolding of our own stories. Each portal is an invitation to pause, reflect, and step consciously into the flow of life.

The work of engaging with temporal portals is not merely about accessing heightened energies but about cultivating a deeper relationship with time itself. It is an act of alignment, a way of harmonizing with the rhythms that govern existence. In doing so, one transcends the mundane constraints of clock and calendar, stepping into a timeless space where the emanations of past, present, and future converge.

Temporal portals are the hinges of transformation, moments where the veil thins and the flow of energy intensifies. To step through them is to participate in the great dance of the cosmos, to feel the currents of existence moving through and around you. They remind us that time is not merely something to be counted but something to be lived, celebrated, and honored as the carrier of life's sacred flows.

Chapter 7
The Invisible Web

Beneath the surface of what is seen lies a vast and intricate web, binding every particle, every being, and every thought into a unified whole. This invisible web is not merely a poetic metaphor but an undeniable reality, vibrating with the currents of emanations that flow through all existence. It is the connective tissue of the universe, a network where energy, intention, and consciousness intermingle, shaping the world in ways both subtle and profound.

The ancient seers, unencumbered by the veil of modern distractions, perceived this web with startling clarity. They described it as the fabric of creation, woven from threads of light, sound, and vibration. Indigenous traditions speak of it as the web of life, where all beings are linked in a symbiotic dance. To touch one strand is to send ripples through the whole, a truth that echoes in the scientific concept of quantum entanglement.

In the natural world, the web reveals itself in myriad forms. The mycelial networks beneath forests connect trees in silent communication, sharing nutrients and information. The murmuration of birds, the synchronized movements of schools of fish, and the migrations of animals all hint at an unseen guidance, a flow that moves beyond individual will. These phenomena are not mere instinct but manifestations of the energetic web that binds all life.

Ancient texts from diverse traditions capture the essence of this web in their own languages. The Vedic sages described *Akasha*, the ether that pervades and connects everything. In Chinese philosophy, the concept of *qi* flows not only within the body but also through the external environment, creating an interconnected system of balance. Indigenous peoples of the Americas speak of the Great Spirit that flows through the earth, sky, and every living thing, forming an indivisible whole.

In the scientific realm, discoveries in quantum physics have begun to affirm what the ancients long understood. The phenomenon of quantum entanglement demonstrates that particles separated by vast distances remain interconnected, their states inexplicably linked. Nonlocality, a principle where events in one location affect those in another without direct contact, mirrors the ancient idea of a web where every thread is tied to the rest.

Studies on morphogenetic fields, proposed by biologist Rupert Sheldrake, further illuminate this interconnectedness. These fields suggest that patterns of behavior, learning, and form are influenced by a collective memory, an energetic blueprint that transcends physical boundaries. A flock of birds, for instance, moves as one not because of individual decision-making but through the influence of this shared field.

Human beings, too, are part of this invisible web. The energy fields that surround and permeate the body—often referred to as the aura or biofield—are not isolated but interact constantly with the environment and others. Emotions, thoughts, and intentions ripple through the web, creating effects far beyond their origin. Modern experiments in intention and consciousness, such as those conducted by the Global Consciousness Project, suggest that collective human focus can influence physical reality, reinforcing the idea of an interconnected energetic network.

Yet, the web is not merely a theoretical construct—it is a lived reality, accessible to those who attune themselves to its subtle vibrations. Practices like meditation, prayer, and energy work serve as portals to this deeper connection. By quieting the mind and expanding awareness, one can begin to feel the threads of the web, sensing the flows of energy that move through and around them.

The invisible web also plays a pivotal role in healing and transformation. Many ancient and modern therapeutic modalities are rooted in the understanding that dis-ease arises from disruptions in the web. Acupuncture, for example, restores balance by addressing blockages in the meridians, the pathways of *qi*. Similarly, practices like Reiki and Healing Touch work to harmonize the body's energy fields, reweaving the threads of the web to promote health and vitality.

Sacred sites, too, are focal points of this web. Ley lines, the invisible currents of earth energy, intersect at these locations, creating vortices where the flow of emanations is amplified. The pyramids of Giza, Stonehenge, and the temples of Angkor Wat are not merely architectural wonders but energetic beacons, attuned to the greater currents of the cosmos. Those who visit these sites often describe a profound sense of connection, as though stepping into the very heart of the web.

For those seeking to consciously navigate the invisible web, practices of perception and intention become essential. Exercises for expanded awareness—such as grounding, visualization, and breathwork—attune one's senses to the subtle flows. Techniques for energy exchange, including giving and receiving through conscious intention, foster a deeper connection to the web and its currents.

The invisible web is also a mirror, reflecting the interconnectedness of inner and outer worlds. As within, so without: the thoughts, emotions, and intentions of an individual ripple through the web, influencing not only their own reality but the collective field. This principle underscores the importance of cultivating harmony within, as it reverberates outward into the greater whole.

Collective consciousness, a manifestation of the web, offers a powerful example of its potential. Moments of global focus—whether through prayer, meditation, or shared intention—demonstrate the web's capacity to amplify and unify energy. Events such as synchronized meditations for peace have shown measurable effects on conflict and violence, suggesting that humanity's collective efforts can shift the energetic tides of the world.

Yet, the web is not without its challenges. Modern life, with its emphasis on individuality and materialism, often blinds people to their place within the greater network. Disconnection from nature, over-reliance on technology, and the fragmentation of communities fray the threads that bind humanity to the web. Restoring this connection requires conscious effort, a return to practices that honor the interconnectedness of all things.

The invisible web, though unseen, is ever-present, a reminder of the unity underlying apparent diversity. To perceive it is to recognize that no action, thought, or being exists in isolation. Every ripple affects the whole, every strand contributes to the strength of the fabric.

In this awareness lies a profound responsibility. By acting with intention, cultivating harmony, and nurturing connection, one can weave a stronger, more vibrant web. The invisible threads of existence become not just a backdrop but a living, breathing presence, guiding and supporting all who move within them.

The web calls to those who would listen, its currents humming with the resonance of life itself. To step into its flow is to awaken to the truth of unity, to see the self not as separate but as an integral thread in the infinite tapestry of creation. It is a journey both inward and outward, a path toward wholeness that begins and ends within the web's infinite embrace.

Chapter 8
Universal Vibration

At the heart of existence lies a simple yet profound truth: everything vibrates. From the hum of a distant star to the whisper of a single atom, the universe is a symphony of vibrations, a continuum of frequencies resonating through time and space. This universal vibration is not merely a concept but the essence of all emanations, the foundation upon which matter, energy, and consciousness are built.

Ancient wisdom traditions understood this principle long before the advent of modern science. In the Vedic scriptures, the concept of *Nada Brahma*—"the world is sound"—describes the universe as a vibration emanating from the primordial *Om*. In Chinese philosophy, *qi* is depicted not as a static force but as a dynamic flow of vibratory energy. Indigenous peoples around the world, from the Aboriginal Australians to the shamans of Siberia, describe the songlines of the earth, pathways of vibrational resonance that connect the land and the cosmos.

Modern physics echoes these ancient insights. Quantum mechanics reveals that particles are not solid entities but oscillations in energy fields, their behavior governed by vibratory patterns. String theory takes this concept further, proposing that the fundamental building blocks of the universe are not particles but vibrating strings of energy. This convergence of ancient and modern thought points to a profound unity: that vibration is the universal language of existence.

Every frequency carries a unique signature, a pattern that defines its expression. In the physical world, this is evident in sound waves, light waves, and electromagnetic fields. The vibrations of sound create music, the vibrations of light produce color, and the vibrations of molecules generate heat. Beyond the physical, vibrations shape emotions, thoughts, and spiritual states, their frequencies influencing the subtler dimensions of being.

Cymatics, the study of visible sound vibration, offers a striking glimpse into this hidden reality. When sound waves pass through a medium such as water or sand, they create intricate patterns, revealing the geometry of vibration. These forms—circles, spirals, and complex fractals—mirror the patterns found in nature, from the petals of a flower to the spiral arms of galaxies. They are a testament to the creative power of vibration, shaping the material world from the unseen.

In the human body, vibration manifests as a constant interplay of energies. The heart generates an electromagnetic field that extends far beyond the physical body, its rhythms influenced by thoughts and emotions. The brain, too, oscillates at specific frequencies, each state of consciousness—waking, dreaming, meditative—corresponding to distinct brainwave patterns. These vibrations are not isolated; they interact with the environment and others, creating a web of energetic exchange.

The chakras, energy centers described in the Vedic tradition, are hubs of vibrational resonance. Each chakra corresponds to a specific frequency and governs different aspects of physical, emotional, and spiritual well-being. When these centers are balanced, their vibrations harmonize, creating a state of coherence within the body and mind. Conversely, disruptions in these frequencies manifest as physical ailments, emotional imbalances, or spiritual disconnection.

Healing traditions across cultures have long worked with vibration to restore balance. In sound healing, instruments like gongs, singing bowls, and tuning forks generate frequencies that resonate with the body's energy fields, dissolving blockages and promoting harmony. The chanting of mantras, such as the sacred *Om*, generates vibrations that align with the cosmic frequency, fostering a sense of unity and transcendence.

Color, too, is a form of vibration, its frequencies interacting with the body and mind in subtle ways. Chromotherapy, the use of color for healing, draws upon this principle, using specific hues to stimulate or calm different energy centers. Red, with its low frequency, energizes and grounds, while blue, with its higher frequency, soothes and inspires.

Beyond healing, vibration serves as a gateway to expanded consciousness. Practices such as breathwork, drumming, and dance induce altered states by modulating the body's rhythms, synchronizing them with higher frequencies. These states open pathways to the unseen, allowing practitioners to perceive the flows of emanations and connect with the universal vibration.

Research into binaural beats and brainwave entrainment offers a contemporary perspective on these practices. By exposing the brain to specific frequencies, these methods influence neural activity, promoting states of relaxation, focus, or deep meditation. Studies suggest that such techniques can enhance creativity, reduce stress, and even foster spiritual experiences, demonstrating the profound impact of vibration on the mind.

The power of vibration extends beyond the individual, shaping collective realities. When groups come together in shared intention—chanting, meditating, or praying—their combined frequencies create a field of resonance that amplifies their energy. This principle underlies practices such as group healing and global meditations, where the vibrations of many converge to generate profound shifts in consciousness.

In nature, vibration reveals itself as a unifying force. The resonant frequencies of the earth, known as the Schumann resonances, align with human brainwaves, creating a subtle yet profound connection between the planet and its inhabitants. The rhythmic patterns of the tides, the cycles of the moon, and the pulsations of stars all reflect the vibratory essence of existence, reminding humanity of its place within the greater web.

To work with universal vibration is to engage with the very fabric of life. Practices that cultivate awareness of vibration—such as chanting, toning, and sound meditation—tune the individual to the frequencies of the cosmos. Visualization exercises, where one imagines waves of light or sound moving through the body, foster a deeper connection to the flow of emanations.

Attuning to vibration also involves cultivating sensitivity to its presence in everyday life. The tone of a voice, the rhythm of a heartbeat, the cadence of a conversation—all carry vibrational signatures that influence perception and interaction. By becoming aware of these subtleties, one can navigate the energetic currents with greater clarity and intention.

The universal vibration is not a distant concept but an intimate reality, humming through every cell, thought, and moment. It is the thread that binds the individual to the infinite, the pulse that animates the cosmos. To feel its presence is to awaken to the truth of interconnectedness, to recognize that all of existence is a single, resonant symphony.

In this symphony, each being plays a note, each moment a chord. The vibrations of one ripple through the whole, creating harmonies and dissonances that shape the unfolding of reality. By tuning oneself to the universal vibration, one becomes a conscious participant in this great dance, co-creating the melodies of existence with every thought, action, and breath.

The universal vibration is both origin and destination, the essence of all emanations and the key to understanding their flow. It is the hum of creation, the song of the cosmos, and the heartbeat of life itself—a reminder that in the vast, resonant web of existence, nothing truly stands apart.

Chapter 9
The Echoes of Creation

The echoes of creation reverberate through the fabric of existence, carrying the memory of every event, thought, and intention. These subtle imprints ripple through time and space, leaving traces that linger in places, objects, and even within the human soul. To perceive these echoes is to hear the whispers of the past, to understand that nothing is truly lost but woven into the infinite tapestry of emanations.

In the mystical traditions of the world, these echoes are described as records, fields, or memories held within the energetic fabric of the universe. The Akashic Records, a concept originating from Hindu and Theosophical thought, are said to be a metaphysical library containing every experience of every soul. This idea resonates with the belief in ancestral memory, the notion that the deeds and wisdom of those who came before are encoded within us, accessible through deep reflection or spiritual practice.

Indigenous cultures speak of the land as a keeper of stories, its stones, rivers, and mountains bearing witness to the lives and energies of those who walked before. Aboriginal Australians, through their Dreamtime stories, describe songlines as paths imbued with ancestral energies, guiding present generations and connecting them to their origins. Similarly, the Navajo people honor the sacred landscapes of their homeland, believing these places hold the echoes of creation and the voices of their ancestors.

Science offers intriguing parallels to these spiritual concepts. Research into quantum mechanics suggests that information, once created, can never truly be destroyed. The principle of quantum memory posits that particles retain traces of their interactions, creating a kind of energetic record. This aligns with theories of morphogenetic fields, proposed by Rupert Sheldrake, which suggest that patterns of behavior and form are influenced by collective memory fields that transcend time and space.

One of the most tangible manifestations of these echoes is the energetic imprint left on places and objects. Spaces where intense emotions have been felt—be it joy, sorrow, or fear—carry a residual energy that sensitive individuals can perceive. These imprints, often called "hauntings" in folklore, are not mere superstitions but expressions of the lingering vibrations left by human experiences.

Sacred sites across the world bear powerful echoes of creation. From the megalithic stones of Avebury to the temples of Angkor Wat, these locations resonate with the energy of those who built and worshiped within them. Visitors often describe feeling a profound sense of connection or timelessness, as though stepping into a space where the veil between past and present is thin.

Objects, too, carry echoes. Heirlooms passed down through generations seem to hum with the memories of those who held them. Tools, jewelry, and even clothing can retain the energetic imprints of their owners, serving as conduits for connection to their stories. Psychometry, the practice of sensing the history of an object through touch, draws upon this principle, revealing how vibrations linger within matter.

To engage with these echoes is to open oneself to the flows of energy that transcend the limitations of linear time. Techniques for accessing these memories vary across traditions but share common themes: deep stillness, focused intention, and receptivity to subtle signals. Meditation and visualization exercises can attune the practitioner to the vibrations of a space or object, allowing its story to emerge.

Environmental readings, a practice found in shamanic traditions, involve entering a space with heightened awareness, sensing its energies, and interpreting its imprints. Rituals, such as smudging or sound cleansing, are often performed to transform stagnant or negative echoes, realigning the space with harmonious vibrations.

The echoes of creation also reside within the human soul, carried as both light and shadow. The concept of karmic memory, prevalent in Eastern philosophy, suggests that the actions and intentions of past lives shape the vibratory patterns of the present. Ancestral memories, passed down through DNA and subtle energetic channels, influence behavior, beliefs, and even physical traits.

Modern science supports this notion through the study of epigenetics, which reveals how experiences—particularly those of stress or trauma—can alter the expression of genes and be transmitted across generations. These findings lend credence to the idea that the echoes of our ancestors live within us, shaping our lives in ways both visible and unseen.

Healing these imprints requires awareness and intention. Practices such as ancestral healing rituals, guided regressions, and inner journeying allow individuals to confront and transform the echoes that no longer serve them. By acknowledging and releasing these energies, one not only frees oneself but also contributes to the healing of the greater web of life.

Beyond healing, the echoes of creation offer profound opportunities for growth and understanding. By tuning into these energies, one can draw upon the wisdom of the past, using it as a guide for navigating the present. The resonance of ancient truths, carried forward in myths, rituals, and sacred teachings, reminds humanity of its enduring connection to the origins of existence.

This process of attunement also fosters a deeper connection to the earth and its rhythms. By listening to the land, observing its flows, and honoring its sacred spaces, one can align with the echoes of creation that permeate the natural world. Such practices not only enhance personal awareness but also cultivate a sense of stewardship, a recognition of one's role as a caretaker of the earth's energies.

The echoes of creation are not confined to the past—they ripple forward, influencing the present and shaping the future. Every thought, word, and action contributes to this ever-expanding tapestry, leaving its mark upon the web of existence. In this sense, humanity becomes both the inheritor and the creator of these echoes, a bridge between what has been and what will be.

To live in awareness of these echoes is to move through the world with reverence, recognizing that every moment is part of a greater whole. It is to listen to the silent songs of the stones, the whispers of the wind, and the stories carried by the stars. It is to honor the threads of connection that bind all things, weaving one's own vibratory patterns into the infinite symphony of creation.

The echoes of creation remind us that nothing is ever truly lost. They are the resonance of the eternal, a testament to the unity and continuity of all existence. To hear them is to awaken to the profound truth that the past, present, and future are but different notes in the same universal melody—a melody that began with the first breath of creation and continues to evolve with every heartbeat, every step, and every whisper of the soul.

Chapter 10
Parallel Dimensions

The universe is far more vast and layered than it appears, a realm not limited to the three-dimensional world we navigate daily. Beneath the surface of what we perceive lies a complex structure of parallel dimensions, subtle planes of existence where the flows of emanations take on forms and movements beyond the grasp of ordinary senses. These dimensions are not distant or unreachable; they intertwine with our own, shaping reality and offering gateways to deeper understanding.

From the earliest myths to the latest scientific theories, humanity has sought to comprehend the existence of parallel dimensions. Ancient spiritual traditions describe these realms as accessible through altered states of consciousness, ritual, or divine intervention. Modern science, through concepts such as string theory and multiverse hypotheses, explores the possibility of countless dimensions existing simultaneously, each vibrating at its unique frequency.

The idea of parallel dimensions is not new. In the Vedic tradition, the concept of *lokas* outlines multiple planes of existence, each with distinct characteristics and inhabitants. The *astras*—celestial realms—are said to vibrate at higher frequencies, home to beings of light and wisdom, while the *patala lokas*—lower realms—reflect denser, shadowy energies. These planes are not separated by distance but by vibration, accessible through spiritual practices that elevate consciousness.

In shamanic traditions, parallel dimensions are known as the upper, middle, and lower worlds. The shaman, acting as a bridge between realms, journeys into these dimensions to retrieve guidance, healing, or wisdom. The lower world, far from being malevolent, is viewed as a source of primal knowledge, a place of grounding and connection with ancestral spirits. The upper world, by contrast, is a realm of light and clarity, where higher beings offer insight and inspiration.

Western esoteric traditions describe the astral plane, a dimension closely interwoven with the physical world. This is the realm of dreams, imagination, and the subtle body, where the vibrations of thoughts and emotions manifest as forms. Mystics and occultists have long used techniques such as astral projection to explore this plane, perceiving it as a vibrant, ever-changing landscape shaped by the currents of intention and energy.

Science, though often skeptical of metaphysical claims, has begun to approach the concept of parallel dimensions through theories that stretch the boundaries of understanding. String theory proposes that beyond the three spatial dimensions and one temporal dimension familiar to us, there exist additional dimensions compacted into imperceptibly small spaces. These hidden dimensions, though beyond direct observation, influence the fundamental forces of nature, shaping the structure of reality itself.

Quantum mechanics, with its principle of superposition and the enigmatic behavior of entangled particles, suggests a universe where multiple possibilities coexist. The many-worlds interpretation posits that every decision, every quantum event, creates a branching of realities, each representing a different outcome. These parallel universes are not distant or separate but layered within the same fabric of existence, each vibrating at its own frequency.

To engage with parallel dimensions is to expand one's awareness beyond the limits of the material world. Meditation, breathwork, and altered states of consciousness serve as portals to these realms, shifting the practitioner's vibration to align with the subtle energies of other planes. Visualization techniques, where one imagines stepping through a doorway or ascending a spiral staircase, guide the mind and spirit into these dimensions.

Dreams, too, are a natural gateway to parallel dimensions. In lucid dreaming, where the dreamer becomes aware of their state, the boundaries between the physical and astral dissolve. The dreamscape, far from being a mere figment of the imagination, often reflects the flows of energy and intention that shape the unseen realms. Many who have mastered lucid dreaming report encounters with beings, places, and insights that feel profoundly real, as though touching another layer of existence.

Shamanic journeying provides another pathway into parallel dimensions. Using rhythmic drumming or other repetitive sounds, the practitioner enters a trance state, their consciousness traveling into the subtle planes. Here, they may encounter spirit guides, animal totems, or archetypal energies, each a manifestation of the vibrations that govern these realms.

The interplay between dimensions is not merely theoretical; it has practical implications for healing and spiritual growth. Energetic imbalances in the physical body often originate in the subtle planes, where stagnant or misaligned vibrations create disharmony. By addressing these issues on the astral or etheric level, practitioners can restore balance and vitality to the physical form.

Parallel dimensions also serve as reservoirs of creativity and inspiration. Many artists, writers, and inventors describe moments of sudden clarity or insight, as though tapping into a source beyond their own mind. These flashes of genius often feel like transmissions from another realm, where ideas and possibilities exist in their purest form.

Yet, the exploration of parallel dimensions demands discernment. Not all energies encountered in these realms are benevolent, and the untrained traveler may encounter vibrations that disrupt rather than harmonize. Protective practices, such as grounding and setting clear intentions, are essential for navigating these spaces safely.

The existence of parallel dimensions also invites reflection on the nature of reality itself. If the universe is a multilayered construct of vibrating energies, then the material world is but one expression of a far more complex and dynamic whole. This perspective dissolves the illusion of separateness, revealing a cosmos where all planes are interconnected, each influencing the other in an intricate dance of emanations.

The awareness of parallel dimensions fosters a deeper connection to the unseen currents that shape life. It reminds us that the boundaries we perceive are not fixed but fluid, that the walls between worlds are as thin as thought. To engage with these dimensions is to step into a broader, more vibrant reality, one where the possibilities of existence expand beyond imagination.

Through this exploration, the self is revealed not as a solitary being but as a multidimensional presence, woven into the fabric of infinite realms. The journey into parallel dimensions is not an escape from the physical but a return to the wholeness of existence, a recognition that the universe is a vast, interconnected web of energy, vibrating with the echoes of countless worlds.

Parallel dimensions are not elsewhere; they are here, layered within and around us, waiting to be perceived. To touch them is to awaken to the truth that reality is not a single path but a boundless expanse, each dimension a thread in the infinite tapestry of creation. They remind us that existence is not limited to what can be seen or measured but extends into the unseen, the uncharted, and the unimaginable—a mystery both humbling and profound.

Chapter 11
The Heart's Field

At the center of the human experience lies the heart—not merely as a biological organ but as a profound energetic center that bridges the physical and spiritual realms. Known across traditions as the seat of the soul, the heart emanates a powerful electromagnetic field that influences the body, mind, and beyond. This field, intricate and dynamic, serves as a central force within the web of emanations, shaping and responding to the subtle energies of existence.

Scientific research has begun to illuminate the heart's energetic power. Studies by the HeartMath Institute reveal that the electromagnetic field generated by the heart is much larger and stronger than that of the brain, extending several feet beyond the body. This field is not static; it changes in response to emotions, thoughts, and interactions with others, acting as both a transmitter and receiver of energetic information.

Ancient wisdom anticipated these findings. In the Upanishads, the heart is described as the dwelling place of the divine spark, a microcosm of the universal essence. Sufism speaks of *qalb*, the spiritual heart, as a vessel for divine love and illumination. The Egyptians revered the heart as the locus of truth, weighing it against the feather of Ma'at in the afterlife to determine the purity of the soul.

These traditions align in their portrayal of the heart as more than a physical center; it is an energetic nucleus through which life's emanations flow. It connects the individual to themselves, to others, and to the greater whole, acting as a bridge between the earthly and the cosmic.

The concept of coherence, both scientific and spiritual, offers insight into the heart's field. Heart coherence occurs when the heart's rhythms synchronize harmoniously, creating a state of energetic alignment within the body. This state fosters emotional balance, cognitive clarity, and a deeper connection to intuition. Techniques to cultivate heart coherence, such as breath-focused meditation and gratitude practices, demonstrate that the heart is not merely reactive but can be consciously attuned.

One of the heart's most profound abilities is its role in energetic communication. Through its electromagnetic field, the heart connects individuals, creating subtle energetic exchanges that influence emotions and perceptions. Studies show that the heart's rhythms synchronize during moments of empathy, love, or shared focus, suggesting that connection transcends words, occurring at the level of vibration.

Ancient practices harnessed this knowledge to foster collective harmony. In group meditations, rituals, and ceremonies, participants aligned their hearts' energies, amplifying their collective field and creating a resonance that extended outward. Modern experiments echo these practices, with global meditations demonstrating measurable effects on collective stress and conflict.

The heart's field also acts as a conduit for transformation. Emotions such as love, compassion, and forgiveness elevate its vibrations, expanding the field and aligning it with higher frequencies. Conversely, emotions such as fear, anger, and resentment constrict the field, disrupting its harmony. This dynamic reflects the interplay of light and shadow, where the heart becomes a microcosm of the broader energetic dance.

Practices to strengthen the heart's field emphasize cultivating positive emotional states. Gratitude journaling, loving-kindness meditation, and heart-centered breathing techniques shift the heart's vibrations, fostering resilience and enhancing its ability to influence the surrounding energetic environment. These practices are not merely internal; their effects ripple outward, creating waves of coherence that touch others and the greater web of life.

The connection between the heart and the brain offers further insight into its energetic role. Neural pathways linking the heart and brain reveal a constant exchange of information, with the heart sending more signals to the brain than it receives. This interplay influences not only emotional and mental states but also perceptions of reality. The heart's intuitive wisdom often precedes cognitive processing, guiding decisions and fostering deeper understanding.

In many spiritual traditions, the heart is described as a portal to higher dimensions of consciousness. In yogic practices, the *anahata* chakra, or heart center, is a gateway to universal love and divine connection. Sufi mystics speak of polishing the heart to reflect the light of the divine, transforming it into a mirror of higher truths. These metaphors emphasize the heart's role as a bridge between the individual and the infinite.

The heart's field also serves as a powerful tool for healing, both personal and collective. Energetic healing modalities, such as Reiki, emphasize the role of the heart in channeling and directing energy. Practitioners often describe the heart as the source of their healing power, radiating vibrations that harmonize and restore balance in others.

Collectively, the heart's field offers a model for transformation on a global scale. By fostering heart-centered practices and cultivating coherence, humanity can create a resonance that transcends divisions, harmonizing the collective field and fostering unity. This principle underpins movements for peace, where shared intention and focus radiate through the heart's field, creating ripples of change.

To engage with the heart's field is to enter a profound relationship with oneself and the universe. Practical techniques deepen this connection:

Heart-focused meditation: Concentrating on the heart while visualizing a radiant light expanding outward fosters coherence and connection.

Emotional awareness practices: Recognizing and transforming negative emotions into positive vibrations enhances the heart's resonance.

Heart-to-heart communication: Holding space for genuine connection with others, whether through listening or shared silence, strengthens energetic bonds.

The heart's field is not merely an abstract concept; it is a lived reality, accessible through intention and awareness. By attuning to its vibrations, one can navigate life with greater clarity, compassion, and purpose. The heart becomes a compass, guiding the self through the flows of emanations and toward alignment with the greater whole.

Through the lens of the heart, the universe reveals itself as a symphony of interconnected energies, each vibration contributing to the whole. The heart's field is a reminder that existence is not a solitary experience but a shared journey, where every beat resonates through the infinite web of life.

The heart's wisdom lies not in complexity but in simplicity—the power to love, to connect, and to transform. It is the seat of truth, the source of life's most profound emanations, and the bridge between the self and the cosmos. By living from the heart, one aligns with the rhythm of creation, embodying the harmony that pulses through all things.

Chapter 12
The Paths of Water

Among the primal elements, water stands as a profound conductor and transmitter of energy, a dynamic force that shapes the physical world while carrying the essence of subtle emanations. Flowing from mountain springs to vast oceans, descending as rain and rising as vapor, water follows a cycle that mirrors the eternal rhythms of life itself. It is not merely a resource but a living conduit for connection, healing, and transformation, imbued with memory and shaped by intention.

In ancient traditions, water was revered as sacred, a medium through which the divine communicated with the material world. Rivers were seen as lifelines of the earth, lakes as mirrors of the heavens, and springs as sources of renewal and vitality. These beliefs were not symbolic but deeply practical, recognizing water's unique ability to absorb, store, and transmit energies and information.

Modern science has begun to affirm these ancient insights. The groundbreaking work of Masaru Emoto revealed how water responds to intention and vibration. Through his experiments, Emoto demonstrated that water exposed to positive words, prayers, or harmonious music formed intricate, beautiful crystalline patterns when frozen. Conversely, water exposed to negative influences produced chaotic, disordered forms. These findings suggest that water is far more than a chemical compound—it is a medium of consciousness, reflecting and amplifying the energies it encounters.

Water's role as a carrier of memory extends beyond human influence. Flowing through rocks, soil, and the roots of plants, it absorbs minerals, nutrients, and energetic imprints from the earth itself. Ancient cultures recognized this connection, using water in rituals to honor the spirits of the land. In shamanic practices, sacred wells and springs were seen as gateways to other realms, their waters offering both physical sustenance and spiritual insight.

The ability of water to transmit emanations is also evident in its use in purification and healing rituals. Across traditions, water is employed to cleanse the body, mind, and spirit, washing away stagnation and restoring balance. The act of immersion, whether in the form of baptism, mikvah, or a sacred bath, symbolizes a return to the source, a reattunement to the flow of life's energies.

Water's vibrational properties make it a powerful amplifier for intention. Indigenous healers often bless water before using it in ceremonies, infusing it with prayers and focused energy. In the Vedic tradition, offerings of water, or *jal*, are made to deities and ancestors, acknowledging its role as a bridge between realms. This practice reflects a universal understanding: that water is not only receptive but also transformative, capable of carrying human intention to the subtle planes.

The concept of water memory, though still debated in mainstream science, resonates with these traditions. Researchers exploring homeopathy suggest that water retains an imprint of substances it has been in contact with, even after dilution beyond measurable presence. This phenomenon, if validated, points to water's extraordinary ability to act as a recorder of information, echoing the ancient belief in its sacred properties.

In spiritual practices, water is often paired with sound, another carrier of vibration. Singing bowls, gongs, and mantras chanted near water create ripples that merge with its flow, enhancing its vibrational potency. This union of water and sound amplifies the healing potential of both, creating a resonance that touches the physical and energetic dimensions.

The ecology of water also reveals its role in the web of emanations. Streams and rivers connect ecosystems, distributing life-sustaining nutrients while shaping landscapes over millennia. This flow mirrors the movement of energy within and between beings, a reminder of the interconnectedness of all life. The health of water systems reflects the health of the larger web, underscoring the importance of honoring and protecting this vital element.

Practical techniques for working with water's energies abound, inviting a deeper relationship with its flows:

Water Meditation: Sitting by a flowing river, a still lake, or even a bowl of water, one can attune to its rhythm, using its gentle movement to quiet the mind and align with the flow of life.

Infusing Water with Intention: Holding a vessel of water while focusing on a specific intention imbues it with energy. Drinking or using this water in rituals strengthens the connection between thought and action.

Sacred Bathing: Immersing oneself in water infused with herbs, salts, or essential oils creates a space for energetic cleansing and renewal. This practice, often accompanied by prayer or visualization, allows one to release stagnant energies and absorb revitalizing vibrations.

Water also serves as a teacher, embodying qualities essential to spiritual growth. Its adaptability, flowing around obstacles and filling any container, reflects the power of surrender and resilience. Its ability to carve canyons and wear down stone reminds us of the strength found in persistence.

Yet, water's role extends beyond the personal to the collective. Ceremonies to honor and heal water—such as those performed by Indigenous water protectors—address not only environmental concerns but also the spiritual disconnection that underlies them. By blessing and caring for water, these rituals restore harmony to the energetic web, acknowledging humanity's responsibility as stewards of the earth's resources.

Water's cycles mirror the cycles of emanations, endlessly renewing and transforming. The rain that falls to the earth, the streams that flow to the sea, and the vapor that rises to the heavens create a continuous loop, a reminder that energy, too, is never lost but constantly evolving. This eternal movement connects the microcosm of individual life to the macrocosm of the universe, a dance of transformation that sustains all existence.

The paths of water invite us to move with its flow, to recognize its wisdom and honor its role as a carrier of life's emanations. By deepening our relationship with water, we attune to the rhythms of the earth and the subtle currents that shape our lives.

In its stillness, water reflects; in its movement, it transforms. Through its paths, it carries the echoes of creation and the promise of renewal. To walk these paths is to embrace the flow of life itself, aligning with the energies that connect us to one another, to the earth, and to the infinite.

Chapter 13
Ancestral Memories

Deep within the fabric of human existence lies a reservoir of echoes—memories carried not in books or monuments but in the currents of energy that flow through generations. These ancestral memories form an invisible thread, connecting the present to the past and shaping the emanations that guide individuals and communities. They are not confined to the mind or even the body but extend into the subtle layers of existence, preserved and transmitted through the energetic web of life.

Ancient traditions recognized the profound influence of these inherited energies. Across cultures, the concept of ancestral lineage carries both spiritual and practical significance. In African cosmologies, ancestors are venerated as active participants in the lives of the living, offering guidance and protection. The Chinese practice of ancestor worship, rooted in Confucian and Taoist principles, emphasizes the ongoing relationship between generations, where rituals sustain and honor the flow of vital energy.

The Vedic concept of *pitru dosha* describes the energetic debts owed to ancestors, suggesting that unresolved patterns from the past can manifest as obstacles in the present. Similarly, Indigenous traditions around the world view ancestral energies as both a source of wisdom and a call to heal intergenerational wounds, ensuring harmony within the family and the community.

Modern science offers a striking parallel to these spiritual insights through the field of epigenetics. Studies reveal that experiences—particularly those involving trauma or stress—can leave chemical imprints on DNA, affecting gene expression in descendants. These findings affirm the ancient understanding that ancestral experiences, both positive and negative, are carried forward, influencing the vibrational patterns of future generations.

Ancestral memories are not limited to trauma; they include the strengths, wisdom, and spiritual practices cultivated over centuries. These imprints form an energetic inheritance, a wellspring of potential that individuals can draw upon for resilience, creativity, and growth. However, accessing this inheritance requires awareness and intentionality, as ancestral energies are often buried beneath the surface of conscious experience.

Energetic traditions provide tools for engaging with ancestral memories, offering pathways to uncover and work with these subtle imprints. One such approach is regression, where individuals explore past lives or ancestral connections through meditation or guided visualization. This process often reveals patterns or unresolved energies that influence the present, offering opportunities for healing and transformation.

Rituals for connecting with ancestors are central to many spiritual practices. In Japan, the annual *Obon* festival honors departed loved ones, inviting their spirits to return and share in the family's life. In Mexico, *Día de los Muertos* serves a similar purpose, creating a space where the veil between worlds is lifted, and the living and the dead reconnect. These ceremonies reinforce the flow of energy between generations, ensuring that the bonds of lineage remain strong.

Working with ancestral memories often involves confronting shadows as well as embracing light. Patterns of fear, anger, or disconnection can arise from unresolved ancestral traumas, creating energetic blockages that ripple through the family line. Healing these patterns requires acknowledging their presence, offering compassion, and consciously transforming their vibrational imprint.

Techniques for ancestral healing vary but share common principles of intention, connection, and release:

Meditative Ancestral Journeys: Guided meditations or trance states can facilitate contact with ancestral energies. These journeys often involve visualizing a sacred space where one can meet and communicate with ancestors, seeking guidance or offering forgiveness.

Rituals of Release: Creating ceremonies to acknowledge and release inherited burdens—through fire, water, or symbolic offerings—transforms stagnant energies, allowing them to flow freely once more.

Generational Mapping: Reflecting on family patterns, both emotional and behavioral, reveals recurring themes and opportunities for healing. This process fosters a deeper understanding of the energetic threads woven through one's lineage.

Ancestral connections are not limited to biological lineage; they extend to spiritual lineages and the broader human family. Many traditions teach that one's spiritual teachers and mentors form an energetic ancestry, passing down wisdom and practices that resonate across time. This lineage, too, carries memories and emanations, offering guidance for those who walk the path of spiritual development.

The relationship between ancestral memories and the land also deserves attention. Many cultures believe that the earth itself holds the imprints of those who came before. Sacred sites, often chosen by ancestors for their energetic significance, serve as portals to these memories, allowing individuals to reconnect with their lineage through the land. Pilgrimages to these sites, accompanied by rituals and prayers, activate the flow of ancestral energy, deepening the bond between the self and the collective past.

In working with ancestral memories, one begins to recognize the interplay between personal and collective energies. The struggles and triumphs of one generation ripple forward, shaping the next. By healing inherited wounds and honoring ancestral wisdom, individuals contribute to the evolution of the entire lineage, creating a resonance that extends beyond the boundaries of time and space.

This process of engagement transforms ancestral memories from burdens into blessings. By integrating the lessons of the past, individuals gain access to a wellspring of strength, creativity, and purpose. They become stewards of their lineage, ensuring that its energies flow harmoniously into the future.

Practical steps for cultivating a relationship with ancestral memories include:

Building an Ancestral Altar: Creating a dedicated space with photographs, mementos, or symbols of ancestors provides a focal point for connection and reflection.

Offering Prayers or Intentions: Speaking to ancestors, whether aloud or in thought, strengthens the bond and invites their guidance.

Researching Lineage: Exploring family history, cultural traditions, and ancestral practices deepens understanding and fosters a sense of belonging.

Ancestral memories are not static; they evolve as they are acknowledged and integrated. Each interaction with these energies reshapes their influence, creating new patterns that resonate through the individual and the collective. This dynamic relationship ensures that the flow of emanations remains vibrant, connecting the past, present, and future in an unbroken continuum.

The echoes of ancestral memories remind us that we are never alone. We carry within us the essence of those who walked before, their struggles and triumphs interwoven with our own. By embracing this connection, we honor their legacy and become active participants in the unfolding story of life, adding our own emanations to the infinite tapestry of existence.

To work with ancestral memories is to awaken to the profound truth of interconnectedness, to see oneself not as an isolated being but as a vital thread in the web of lineage and life. It is a path of healing, discovery, and transformation, where the energies of the past illuminate the present and guide the way forward. Through this journey, the bonds of ancestry become a source of strength and inspiration, a reminder that we are all part of a timeless flow, moving together through the vast currents of creation.

Chapter 14
The Cosmic Mind

Beyond the vast expanse of stars and galaxies lies a deeper dimension of existence, one that transcends the physical universe and pulsates with pure consciousness. This is the Cosmic Mind, a universal intelligence that permeates all things, shaping the emanations that give form and meaning to reality. It is the source from which all thoughts, ideas, and creations arise, an infinite reservoir of wisdom and energy that flows through every layer of existence.

Throughout history, spiritual traditions and philosophical systems have sought to understand this profound connection between individual consciousness and the Cosmic Mind. In the Vedic tradition, it is referred to as *Brahman*, the ultimate reality that underpins and unifies the universe. In Hermetic philosophy, it is known as the *Mind of God*, a creative force that manifests the material and immaterial realms. The ancient Greeks spoke of the *Nous*, the divine intellect that orders the cosmos and connects human thought to higher truths.

Modern science, too, has begun to explore the possibility of a universal consciousness. Quantum physics suggests that the universe operates not as a collection of separate entities but as an interconnected whole. Experiments in quantum entanglement reveal that particles, once linked, remain connected regardless of distance, hinting at a deeper unity beneath the surface of reality. Theories of a holographic universe propose that all information is encoded within every part of existence, echoing the ancient idea of the Cosmic Mind as a unified field of knowledge.

The relationship between the Cosmic Mind and individual consciousness is both profound and intimate. Every thought, intention, and perception arises as a ripple within this vast ocean of awareness. Just as a drop of water contains the essence of the sea, human consciousness reflects the infinite wisdom and creativity of the Cosmic Mind. This connection is not metaphorical but literal, as the currents of emanations flow seamlessly between the individual and the universal.

Meditative and contemplative practices have long been used to attune to this connection. Through silence and stillness, practitioners quiet the noise of the ego and open themselves to the subtle frequencies of the Cosmic Mind. In this state, insights arise not as logical conclusions but as sudden, intuitive understandings—moments of clarity that transcend ordinary thought.

The Cosmic Mind is not a passive presence but an active force, constantly shaping and reshaping reality. It is the source of archetypes, the universal symbols that appear across cultures and time, guiding humanity's spiritual evolution. These archetypes, as explored in earlier chapters, are more than patterns; they are expressions of the Cosmic Mind's intelligence, bridges that connect the seen with the unseen, the temporal with the eternal.

Within the Cosmic Mind, time and space lose their linear constraints. Mystical experiences often involve a sense of timelessness, a direct perception of the eternal now. This state, described in spiritual traditions as *samadhi* or unity consciousness, reveals the true nature of the Cosmic Mind as a dimension where all possibilities coexist, where past, present, and future merge into a singular flow.

Accessing the Cosmic Mind requires an expansion of awareness beyond the confines of individuality. Practices such as deep meditation, breathwork, and certain forms of prayer align the practitioner's vibrations with the universal field, creating a resonance that allows for a direct experience of this infinite intelligence. In this state, boundaries dissolve, and the individual becomes a channel through which the emanations of the Cosmic Mind flow freely.

The creative process provides another pathway to connect with the Cosmic Mind. Artists, writers, and inventors often describe moments of inspiration as though ideas emerge fully formed from beyond themselves. This phenomenon, often called a "flow state," reflects the alignment of individual creativity with the universal currents of the Cosmic Mind. Such states are not limited to the gifted; they are accessible to anyone who opens themselves to the deeper rhythms of thought and intention.

The Cosmic Mind also manifests in collective consciousness, the shared field of energy and awareness that connects groups, communities, and even entire species. Phenomena such as mass movements, scientific breakthroughs, and cultural shifts often arise simultaneously across different parts of the world, suggesting an underlying intelligence that guides collective evolution. These synchronicities are not random but expressions of the Cosmic Mind's ability to harmonize and unify disparate elements into a greater whole.

At the heart of this connection lies the principle of resonance. Just as a tuning fork vibrates in harmony with a matching frequency, human consciousness resonates with the vibrations of the Cosmic Mind when aligned through intention and focus. This resonance amplifies the flow of emanations, allowing for a deeper understanding of oneself and the universe.

Practical techniques for cultivating this resonance include:

Meditation on Unity: Focusing on the interconnectedness of all things fosters a direct experience of the Cosmic Mind. Visualizing oneself as a wave within an infinite ocean creates a sense of alignment with the universal field.

Journaling Intuitive Insights: Recording sudden inspirations or seemingly random ideas helps to recognize patterns of connection to the Cosmic Mind's intelligence.

Creative Expression: Engaging in art, music, or writing with a focus on flow rather than outcome opens channels to the

Cosmic Mind, allowing its emanations to manifest through the individual.

The Cosmic Mind is also a source of healing and transformation. By attuning to its wisdom, individuals can access deeper layers of intuition, uncovering the root causes of physical, emotional, and spiritual imbalances. Energetic practices such as Reiki, Qigong, or prayer channel the healing currents of the Cosmic Mind, harmonizing the individual with the universal flow.

Moreover, the Cosmic Mind offers profound guidance in times of uncertainty or crisis. By quieting the reactive mind and listening to the subtle emanations of universal intelligence, one can discern paths forward that align with the greater good. This process requires trust and surrender, a willingness to let go of ego-driven desires and allow the wisdom of the Cosmic Mind to illuminate the way.

As humanity faces collective challenges—climate change, social upheaval, and the search for meaning in a rapidly changing world—the Cosmic Mind emerges as a guiding force. By aligning with its emanations, individuals and communities can tap into solutions that transcend the limitations of isolated thinking. The Cosmic Mind does not impose but invites, offering a vision of unity and coherence that can reshape the trajectory of existence.

To live in harmony with the Cosmic Mind is to awaken to the profound truth of interconnectedness. It is to recognize that every thought, every action, and every being is part of a greater whole, a symphony of vibrations that flows through the infinite web of life. The Cosmic Mind is not distant or abstract; it is present in every breath, every moment, and every expression of existence.

Through the Cosmic Mind, one finds not only answers but also a sense of belonging, a reminder that life's emanations are part of a vast and boundless intelligence. To connect with it is to step into the flow of creation itself, to become a co-creator in the unfolding dance of the universe. In this connection lies the promise of transformation, the realization that the Cosmic Mind is not merely an external force but the essence of what it means to be fully alive.

Chapter 15
Light and Shadow

In the eternal dance of creation, light and shadow move as inseparable forces, weaving the fabric of existence. These dualities are not adversaries but complementary aspects of the same energy, each giving meaning and form to the other. To explore light and shadow is to step into the heart of emanations, where every polarity exists in dynamic balance, shaping the flows of the universe and the soul.

Throughout history, spiritual traditions have embraced the interplay of light and shadow as a fundamental truth. In Taoist philosophy, the *yin* and *yang* symbolize this duality, their opposing yet interconnected forms embodying the harmony of contrasts. Similarly, the Gnostic teachings describe the world as a balance of light and darkness, where understanding one requires embracing the other. This ancient wisdom reflects a profound truth: that shadow is not the absence of light but its partner in creation.

Light has long been associated with consciousness, purity, and the divine. It illuminates paths, reveals truths, and inspires growth. Mystics and sages speak of the "inner light," a radiant emanation that guides the soul toward its highest potential. This light is not confined to the physical world but flows through all dimensions of existence, connecting the individual to the universal.

Yet, where there is light, there is shadow. Shadow represents the hidden, the unknown, and often the feared. It is the space where unacknowledged aspects of the self reside, waiting to be seen and integrated. While the shadow may seem dark and forbidding, it is rich with potential, holding the keys to transformation and wholeness.

Carl Jung, whose work illuminated the shadow's role in human psychology, described it as the "dark side" of the psyche—the parts of ourselves we reject or deny. Yet, he also emphasized its creative and transformative power, suggesting that true self-awareness arises not from escaping the shadow but from integrating it with the light.

This principle extends beyond the individual to the collective. Societies, like individuals, have their shadows—unspoken histories, suppressed truths, and hidden energies that shape their actions and identities. To confront these shadows is to uncover the deeper currents of collective consciousness, opening pathways for healing and renewal.

The interplay of light and shadow is not static but dynamic, a continual process of movement and balance. In the cycles of nature, this duality is evident in the turning of day into night, the waxing and waning of the moon, and the changing of seasons. These rhythms remind us that light and shadow are not fixed states but evolving expressions of energy.

In the human experience, the journey between light and shadow often takes the form of transformation. Moments of clarity and enlightenment arise after periods of struggle and uncertainty, just as dawn follows the darkest hour of night. This pattern reflects the alchemical process of transmutation, where dense and heavy energies are refined into light.

Alchemical traditions, both literal and metaphorical, provide profound insights into working with light and shadow. The transformation of base metals into gold symbolizes the inner process of turning fear, anger, and limitation into wisdom, compassion, and strength. This journey, often called the "Great Work," is not about eliminating shadow but about integrating it into a greater whole.

Practical techniques for engaging with light and shadow include:

Shadow Work: Reflecting on hidden fears, desires, or patterns without judgment allows the shadow to emerge. Journaling, therapy, or meditative inquiry creates space for these aspects to be seen and understood.

Visualization Practices: Imagining light flowing into areas of resistance or pain brings awareness and healing to the shadow's depths. Conversely, visualizing the shadow merging with light fosters integration and balance.

Sacred Rituals: Ceremonies that honor both light and shadow—such as lighting candles in a dark space or invoking opposites in prayer—embody the harmony of these forces.

Rituals tied to celestial events, such as eclipses or solstices, provide powerful opportunities to work with these energies. An eclipse, where light and shadow align, creates a moment of heightened transformation, inviting reflection on what must be embraced or released. Similarly, the solstices, marking the extremes of light and darkness, celebrate the balance inherent in the cycles of existence.

Art and creativity also serve as tools for exploring light and shadow. Through painting, writing, dance, or music, individuals express the unspoken and unseen, giving form to energies that defy words. This act of creation transforms the shadow into something tangible and beautiful, a testament to its power and potential.

Collectively, light and shadow shape the stories we tell about ourselves and the world. Myths and legends often depict heroes who journey into the underworld or face their darkest fears, emerging transformed and empowered. These narratives resonate because they reflect an eternal truth: that growth arises not from avoiding shadow but from meeting it with courage and compassion.

In recognizing the shadow's role, one discovers its gifts. The shadow holds the energy of unfulfilled dreams, unexpressed emotions, and untapped potential. By integrating these aspects, individuals reclaim parts of themselves, becoming more whole and authentic. This process is not easy, but it is essential for living in alignment with the flows of emanations.

The light, too, has its challenges. Over-identification with light can lead to spiritual bypassing, where shadow is ignored or denied in pursuit of an idealized image of purity. This imbalance creates fragility, as the unacknowledged shadow grows stronger in the background. True alignment requires embracing both light and shadow, recognizing their interplay as the essence of life itself.

The duality of light and shadow also mirrors the broader currents of the universe. Stars are born in the darkness of space, their light traveling vast distances to illuminate the void. Black holes, the ultimate expression of shadow, hold immense gravitational power, shaping galaxies and influencing the cosmos. Together, these forces create the structure and beauty of the universe, a reminder that light and shadow are not opposites but partners in creation.

To walk the path of light and shadow is to embrace the fullness of existence. It is to see oneself not as divided but as whole, a being of complexity and depth. By working with these energies, one learns to navigate life with greater awareness, compassion, and strength, flowing with the rhythms of transformation that define the human journey.

In the interplay of light and shadow lies the key to balance, the secret of harmony within the self and the universe. It is a dance of contrasts, a testament to the unity that underlies all duality. To embrace both is to step into the flow of creation, becoming a living expression of the dynamic, ever-changing emanations that shape existence.

Chapter 16
The Inner Labyrinth

Beneath the surface of human consciousness lies a vast and intricate labyrinth, a realm where emanations flow through the corridors of the psyche. This inner maze is not a simple construct of thoughts and memories; it is an ever-shifting landscape of emotions, desires, archetypes, and mysteries. To navigate it is to embark on the profound journey of self-discovery, where each turn reveals both the familiar and the unknown.

The labyrinth of the inner world has been a symbol of transformation across cultures and epochs. In Greek mythology, the labyrinth guarded by the Minotaur represents the journey into the depths of the self, where confronting the shadow unlocks freedom and wisdom. In medieval Europe, labyrinths etched into cathedral floors became tools for meditative walking, their spirals mirroring the soul's path toward union with the divine.

This labyrinth is not a metaphor but a reality, an energetic structure shaped by the interplay of emanations within the human psyche. It is both personal and universal, containing the unique patterns of an individual's life while resonating with the collective archetypes that shape humanity as a whole.

At the heart of the labyrinth lies the self, not as a static identity but as a dynamic force—a center of awareness that reflects and refracts the flows of emanations. This self is neither the ego nor the conscious mind; it is the silent observer, the essence that remains constant amid the flux of thoughts and emotions. To reach this center is to glimpse the source of one's being, to connect with the emanations that pulse through existence.

The labyrinth's paths are shaped by the layers of consciousness. On the surface lies the conscious mind, the realm of rational thought and immediate perception. Below it, the subconscious holds memories, beliefs, and emotions, many of which influence behavior without conscious awareness. Deeper still, the unconscious harbors the shadow, the archetypes, and the collective patterns that connect the individual to the greater whole.

Each layer of the labyrinth offers insights and challenges. The conscious mind, though limited in scope, provides the tools of reason and intention. The subconscious, a reservoir of past experiences and unresolved energies, invites exploration and healing. The unconscious, vast and mysterious, reveals the universal currents that flow through all beings, offering wisdom that transcends the individual.

To navigate the labyrinth is to engage with these layers, to move through its winding paths with curiosity and courage. This journey requires tools and practices that illuminate the inner world, guiding the seeker through its complexities.

One such tool is self-inquiry, the practice of questioning thoughts, emotions, and beliefs to uncover their origins and significance. By asking, "Who am I beyond this thought? What lies beneath this emotion?" the seeker peels back the layers of the psyche, moving closer to the core of their being.

Meditation provides another pathway into the labyrinth. In stillness, the mind becomes a mirror, reflecting the patterns and flows within. Visualization exercises, where one imagines walking through an actual labyrinth, deepen this practice, creating a symbolic journey that mirrors the inner exploration.

Dreamwork offers unique insights into the labyrinth's hidden corners. Dreams, as emanations of the subconscious and unconscious, often contain symbols, archetypes, and messages that reveal the inner dynamics of the psyche. By journaling and reflecting on dreams, one can uncover patterns and themes that guide the journey through the labyrinth.

The labyrinth is also a space of transformation, where stagnant energies can be released and new potentials awakened. Practices such as breathwork and movement therapy activate the flows of emanations within the body, breaking through blockages and restoring harmony. Rituals that honor the shadow, such as lighting a candle in darkness or offering a symbolic object, create space for integration and healing.

The shadow plays a pivotal role in the labyrinth, guarding its deepest passages and most profound treasures. It contains the parts of the self that have been repressed or denied, from unexpressed anger to unacknowledged talents. To face the shadow is not to battle it but to embrace it, recognizing it as an integral part of the whole.

Carl Jung described this process as individuation, the journey toward becoming a complete and integrated self. By acknowledging and integrating the shadow, the seeker transforms its energy into wisdom and power, unlocking the hidden gifts within the labyrinth.

The labyrinth also holds the archetypes, universal patterns that guide and shape human experience. These figures—such as the hero, the mentor, the trickster, and the wise elder—serve as companions and guides within the inner journey. By recognizing their presence, the seeker aligns with the flows of the Cosmic Mind, accessing the wisdom of the collective unconscious.

Practical techniques for working with the archetypes include:

Journaling with Archetypes: Writing dialogues with inner figures, such as a wise mentor or a rebellious trickster, creates a bridge between conscious awareness and archetypal energies.

Artistic Expression: Drawing, painting, or sculpting the archetypes encountered in dreams or meditations gives form to their emanations, making their presence tangible.

Ritual Invocation: Creating ceremonies to honor or engage with specific archetypes deepens the connection to their energies, inviting their guidance and insight.

The labyrinth is not a space to be conquered but a mystery to be embraced. Its winding paths reflect the nonlinear nature of growth and transformation, where progress often feels like a return to familiar ground. Yet, each step deepens the journey, revealing new perspectives and possibilities.

At the labyrinth's center lies not a destination but a moment of profound stillness—a space where the flows of emanations converge, and the self is both lost and found. This center is not a place of finality but a point of balance, a reminder that the journey itself is the essence of transformation.

The inner labyrinth is also a microcosm of the greater web of existence. Just as the paths of the psyche reflect the flows of emanations within, they mirror the currents that move through the cosmos. By navigating the labyrinth, the seeker aligns with these greater flows, attuning to the rhythms of life and creation.

To walk the labyrinth is to embark on the most ancient and universal of journeys—the journey inward, toward the essence of being. It is a path of challenges and revelations, where light and shadow intertwine, and every step brings the seeker closer to the truth of their existence.

In the labyrinth, there are no wrong turns, only opportunities to learn, grow, and transform. Each corridor, each shadowed corner, holds a gift waiting to be uncovered, a reminder of the infinite depths within. By stepping into the labyrinth, the seeker becomes both explorer and creator, weaving their own emanations into the endless flow of life.

Chapter 17
The Roots of the Earth

Beneath the surface of the world lies a living network of energy—roots that extend far beyond the physical, connecting all beings to the pulse of the earth. These terrestrial emanations flow through soil, stone, and life itself, forming a bridge between the material and the spiritual. They are not merely remnants of ancient forests or geological formations but carriers of wisdom, grounding forces that sustain the balance of existence.

From the dawn of humanity, cultures have recognized and revered the energies of the earth. Indigenous traditions often describe the planet as a sentient being, its roots an extension of its lifeforce. In many mythologies, the world tree—a symbol of the earth's connection to the cosmos—embodies the unity of the physical and spiritual realms. Its roots delve deep into the unseen, anchoring the energy of creation while feeding the cycles of life above.

The science of geomagnetic fields and telluric currents offers modern insights into these ancient beliefs. The earth's magnetic field, generated by the movement of molten iron in its core, influences not only physical phenomena but also biological and energetic systems. These geomagnetic flows align with ley lines, the invisible currents that many traditions believe carry the earth's energy across landscapes. Sacred sites such as Stonehenge, Machu Picchu, and the Great Pyramids are often situated along these lines, amplifying the emanations they intersect.

Human beings are inherently connected to these terrestrial energies, their bodies and spirits deeply influenced by the rhythms of the earth. The Schumann resonance, a set of frequencies generated by lightning and the planet's electromagnetic field, aligns closely with human brainwaves, fostering a profound resonance between the earth and its inhabitants. This subtle connection reflects a truth long understood by ancient cultures: that to attune to the earth's roots is to align with the flow of life itself.

Grounding, or earthing, is one of the simplest and most powerful ways to engage with terrestrial emanations. Walking barefoot on soil, sand, or grass allows the body to absorb the earth's electrons, neutralizing stress and promoting balance. This practice, rooted in Indigenous traditions, reconnects individuals to the planet's energy, restoring harmony to both body and mind.

Crystals and minerals, formed deep within the earth's layers, also carry its energetic imprint. Each stone, shaped over millennia, holds a unique vibration that resonates with specific aspects of human experience. Quartz, with its clarity and amplification properties, is often used to focus intentions and magnify energy. Obsidian, formed from volcanic activity, embodies the transformative power of fire and earth, aiding in emotional release and protection.

The roots of the earth are not confined to the physical realm; they extend into the spiritual, offering pathways for connection and healing. Practices such as geomancy and dowsing tap into these energies, using intuition and tools to perceive the flows of the earth's currents. In Feng Shui, the placement of objects and structures aligns with these flows, harmonizing the built environment with the natural world.

Trees, with their deep roots and towering branches, serve as living embodiments of the earth's connection to the cosmos. Their roots anchor them in the soil, drawing nourishment and stability, while their canopies reach skyward, capturing sunlight and rain. To sit beneath a tree is to experience this duality, to feel both grounded and expansive, connected to the earth and the heavens.

Rituals that honor the earth's roots deepen this connection. Planting seeds with intention, creating mandalas from natural materials, or simply spending time in undisturbed wilderness fosters a relationship with the planet's energies. These acts are not merely symbolic; they are participatory, inviting individuals to become co-creators in the earth's cycles.

The concept of roots extends beyond the physical to the ancestral and spiritual. Just as trees are nourished by the soil, individuals are nourished by the energies of those who came before. Ancestral traditions often emphasize the importance of staying grounded in one's heritage while reaching toward personal growth. This balance mirrors the relationship between the roots and branches of a tree, where stability and expansion coexist.

In shamanic practices, the roots of the earth are often viewed as pathways to the underworld, a realm of wisdom, healing, and transformation. Journeys to this realm, guided by drumbeats or other rhythmic tools, allow practitioners to access the deep currents of the earth's energy, seeking guidance and restoration. These journeys are not escapes but returns, a reawakening to the truths embedded within the planet's core.

The ecological crisis of the modern world highlights the urgent need to reconnect with the earth's roots. As humanity becomes increasingly disconnected from the land, the balance of terrestrial emanations is disrupted, leading to environmental and energetic disharmony. Practices that honor the earth—such as rewilding, permaculture, and ritual offerings—help to restore this balance, ensuring that the flows of energy remain vibrant and aligned.

Practical techniques for attuning to the roots of the earth include:

Grounding Exercises: Walking barefoot, meditating outdoors, or lying on the ground allows direct connection with the earth's energy, fostering stability and clarity.

Crystal Work: Holding or placing specific stones on the body enhances the flow of terrestrial emanations, aligning physical and energetic systems.

Nature Immersion: Spending time in forests, mountains, or other natural settings restores the connection to the earth's rhythms, promoting both relaxation and insight.

The roots of the earth are not passive; they are dynamic, alive with the energy of creation. They remind humanity of its place within the web of existence, a part of the greater whole rather than separate from it. By engaging with these roots, individuals tap into a source of strength and wisdom that transcends the limitations of the self.

To honor the roots of the earth is to honor the foundations of life itself. It is to recognize that beneath every step lies a network of energy, connecting the past, present, and future in an unbroken chain. This connection, though often forgotten, is always present, waiting to be felt and nurtured.

In the roots of the earth, one finds grounding and growth, stability and transformation. They are a reminder that life's emanations flow not only upward and outward but also downward and inward, anchoring the self in the vast and vibrant energy of the planet. To walk this path is to return to the source, to feel the pulse of the earth beneath one's feet, and to align with the infinite rhythms of creation.

Chapter 18
Primal Sounds

Before the first word was spoken, before the first melody was sung, the universe hummed with vibration. These primal sounds, the original emanations of existence, are not confined to the audible range of human hearing but encompass the essence of creation itself. Sound, both subtle and powerful, shapes matter and energy, forming the bridge between the material and the spiritual, the seen and the unseen.

Ancient traditions often speak of the universe's origins in sound. In Hindu cosmology, the sacred syllable *Om* is said to be the vibration from which all existence emerged, its resonance encompassing the past, present, and future. Similarly, the Gospel of John proclaims, "In the beginning was the Word," emphasizing the creative power of sound as the foundation of reality. Indigenous peoples across the globe have their own origin stories where the world was sung, chanted, or drummed into being, reflecting a universal reverence for sound as the source of life.

Modern science affirms the transformative power of sound. Cymatics, the study of visible sound vibrations, reveals how specific frequencies create intricate patterns in matter, such as water or sand. These patterns, known as Chladni figures, demonstrate that sound not only moves but also organizes, shaping the physical world into coherent forms. On a larger scale, astrophysical research suggests that the cosmic microwave background—the faint hum left from the Big Bang—contains vibrational echoes of the universe's earliest moments.

In the human experience, sound serves as a carrier of emanations, deeply influencing the body, mind, and spirit. The rhythms of a beating drum can induce trance states, aligning consciousness with the subtle flows of energy. The resonance of a singing bowl or gong can dissolve tension, creating harmony within and without. Even the simple act of humming generates vibrations that stimulate the vagus nerve, promoting relaxation and healing.

The power of sound lies in its ability to penetrate and transform. Unlike light, which can be blocked or refracted, sound moves through barriers, resonating within the spaces it touches. This quality makes sound a profound tool for healing and connection, capable of reaching places that words or actions cannot.

Across cultures, sacred sounds have been used to align with the divine and access higher states of consciousness. Chanting mantras, such as the Vedic *Om Mani Padme Hum* or the Tibetan *Om Ah Hum*, creates vibratory patterns that harmonize the practitioner's energy with the universal flow. In Christian traditions, Gregorian chants serve a similar purpose, their resonant tones lifting the spirit and anchoring the soul in sacred spaces.

Drumming, one of the oldest musical expressions, holds a unique role in connecting individuals to primal energies. In shamanic traditions, the repetitive beat of a drum mirrors the rhythms of the earth, creating a bridge between worlds. This beat, often described as the "heartbeat of the earth," guides practitioners into altered states, where they can perceive and work with emanations in the unseen realms.

The voice, as an instrument of sound, carries a unique power. Singing, chanting, or speaking with intention creates vibrations that shape both the inner and outer worlds. The human voice, imbued with emotion and intention, becomes a channel for energy, capable of healing, inspiring, and transforming. This understanding lies at the heart of practices such as overtone singing, where vocalists produce multiple tones simultaneously, resonating with the harmonics of the universe.

Practical techniques for working with primal sounds include:

Chanting and Mantras: Repeating sacred syllables or phrases focuses the mind and aligns the body's vibrations with higher frequencies. The rhythm and resonance of the chant amplify its effects, creating a flow of energy that permeates the practitioner's being.

Sound Meditation: Sitting in the presence of resonant instruments, such as crystal bowls, gongs, or chimes, allows the body and mind to attune to their frequencies. These meditative practices dissolve tension, restoring balance and clarity.

Vocal Toning: Sustaining a single note with intention, allowing the sound to flow through the body, creates internal resonance that promotes healing and awareness.

The interaction between sound and water offers a compelling demonstration of its transformative potential. Water, which comprises a significant portion of the human body, responds to sound vibrations in profound ways. Experiments by Masaru Emoto revealed that water exposed to positive words or harmonious music formed beautiful crystalline structures, while negative sounds produced chaotic patterns. These findings suggest that sound not only influences but also imprints energy onto matter, shaping the very essence of life.

The planetary scale of sound is equally profound. The earth itself produces low-frequency vibrations known as *infrasound*, often imperceptible to human ears but felt as a deep resonance. These sounds, generated by natural phenomena such as earthquakes, storms, or ocean waves, connect the planet's rhythms to its inhabitants, fostering a subtle but powerful sense of unity.

Celestial bodies, too, emit their own vibratory signatures. The "music of the spheres," an ancient philosophical concept, describes the harmonious frequencies produced by the movements of planets and stars. Modern instruments have captured these sounds, translating them into audible ranges and revealing a cosmos alive with vibration.

The integration of sound into healing practices demonstrates its practical applications. Sound therapy, using tuning forks, singing bowls, or vocal techniques, aligns the body's energy centers, or chakras, restoring their natural frequencies. Music therapy, tailored to individual needs, uses rhythm and melody to support emotional and psychological well-being.

The role of sound in group practices amplifies its power. Collective chanting, drumming, or singing creates a shared resonance that unites participants, dissolving individual boundaries and fostering a sense of connection. These practices, whether in spiritual ceremonies or communal gatherings, harness the primal energy of sound to strengthen collective emanations.

In the personal journey, primal sounds offer guidance and transformation. The act of listening—truly attuning to the vibrations of the world—opens pathways to deeper awareness. Whether it is the rustling of leaves, the song of a bird, or the hum of one's own breath, each sound carries a unique emanation, inviting the listener to engage with the flow of life.

Primal sounds are not confined to sacred spaces or rituals; they are woven into the fabric of existence. The rhythm of footsteps on a forest path, the cadence of waves crashing on a shore, or the hum of a city alive with activity all reflect the emanations of sound in its infinite forms. To attune to these vibrations is to participate in the symphony of creation, to feel the pulse of the universe resonating through every moment.

In the echoes of primal sounds, one discovers a profound truth: that all of existence is vibration, a continuous flow of energy shaped and sustained by the harmonies of the cosmos. By engaging with these sounds, whether through meditation, music, or simple awareness, one taps into the essence of life itself, aligning with the rhythms that connect the self to the infinite.

Primal sounds remind us that the universe is not silent but alive with resonance, each vibration a thread in the intricate web of emanations. To listen is to awaken, to feel the currents of creation moving through the world and within the soul. It is a journey into the origins of being, where sound and silence converge in the eternal dance of existence.

Chapter 19
Elemental Keys

The elements are not mere symbols or abstract concepts; they are the foundation of existence, shaping and defining the flows of energy that animate all life. Each element carries a distinct vibration, a unique emanation that influences both the material and spiritual realms. To work with these elemental keys is to unlock profound truths about the self, the world, and the cosmos, aligning with the primal forces that govern creation and transformation.

From the earliest days of human consciousness, the elements have been revered as sacred. The classical traditions of Greece and India describe them as the building blocks of existence: earth, water, fire, air, and ether. These elements are not separate entities but interconnected aspects of a unified whole, each one expressing a different facet of the same underlying energy. They are at once tangible and intangible, physical and metaphysical, forming the bridge between the visible world and the unseen currents that flow through it.

Earth represents stability, structure, and the grounding force that sustains life. It is the foundation upon which all things rest, the embodiment of endurance and support. Water flows with adaptability and connection, carrying the energy of emotion, intuition, and transformation. Fire burns with intensity and vitality, igniting creation and destruction in its ceaseless dance of renewal. Air moves invisibly yet powerfully, representing thought, communication, and the breath of life. Ether, the most subtle and encompassing element, exists beyond the physical, holding the space for all emanations to manifest and flow.

These elements are not isolated forces but deeply interconnected, constantly interacting to create balance and harmony. The earth needs water to nourish its soil, fire to transform it, air to breathe life into it, and ether to give it purpose. This dynamic interplay mirrors the relationships within the human experience, where physical, emotional, mental, and spiritual aspects must align to create wholeness.

Each element also resonates with specific qualities and energies within the human being. Earth aligns with the body, grounding the self in the present moment. Water flows through the emotions, connecting the inner world to the outer. Fire fuels the will and spirit, sparking creativity and passion. Air breathes life into thoughts and communication, carrying the currents of ideas and understanding. Ether, as the most ethereal of the elements, connects the individual to the infinite, opening pathways to higher awareness and universal consciousness.

Across cultures, the elements have been integrated into spiritual practices, rituals, and philosophies. In Chinese medicine, the five elements—wood, fire, earth, metal, and water—form the foundation of health and balance, their interactions shaping the flows of *qi* within the body. In alchemical traditions, the elements represent stages of transformation, guiding the seeker from the dense material world to the refined realms of spirit. Indigenous cultures around the world honor the elements through ceremonies that invoke their energies, seeking guidance, healing, and harmony.

Working with the elements is a powerful way to attune to the flows of emanations within and around the self. The first step is to cultivate awareness of their presence, observing how they manifest in nature and in one's own experience. The solidity of the earth beneath one's feet, the flow of water in a river or a tear, the warmth of sunlight on the skin, the movement of air through the lungs, and the expansive stillness of ether in the silence between breaths—all are expressions of the elements, inviting connection and reflection.

To deepen this connection, intentional practices can be employed. Meditation on the elements, visualizing each one and its qualities, creates a resonance that aligns the practitioner with their energies. Rituals that honor the elements, such as lighting a candle for fire, pouring water for purification, or placing one's hands on the earth in gratitude, foster a sense of reciprocity and harmony.

The elements also offer guidance in times of imbalance or disconnection. When overwhelmed or scattered, grounding practices that connect to earth restore stability and presence. When emotions stagnate or flow uncontrollably, water rituals bring clarity and balance. When vitality wanes, fire rekindles the inner flame, igniting passion and determination. When thoughts become clouded or communication falters, air clears the mind and carries intention. And when the soul yearns for meaning, ether opens the heart to infinite possibilities.

The elements are not confined to the physical world; they extend into the energetic and spiritual dimensions. In the subtle body, the elements resonate with the chakras, the energy centers that govern different aspects of being. The root chakra vibrates with the stability of earth, the sacral chakra with the fluidity of water, the solar plexus with the power of fire, the heart and throat chakras with the freedom of air, and the crown chakra with the expansiveness of ether. By working with the elements, one can harmonize these centers, enhancing the flow of energy through the body and mind.

The dynamic balance of the elements also mirrors the broader rhythms of nature. The cycles of the seasons reflect their interplay: the growth and abundance of earth in spring, the nurturing rains of water in summer, the transformative fires of autumn, and the cleansing winds of air in winter. Ether holds these cycles within its vastness, uniting them in the endless flow of time.

Engaging with the elements in their natural settings amplifies their energy. Walking barefoot on the earth, swimming in a river or ocean, basking in the warmth of the sun, breathing deeply in open air, and meditating under a star-filled sky all create direct connections to the elements, strengthening their influence and fostering a sense of unity with the greater whole.

The elements also serve as teachers, offering lessons through their presence and behavior. Earth teaches patience and resilience, water adaptability and flow, fire courage and transformation, air freedom and perspective, and ether transcendence and connection. By observing and honoring these qualities, one aligns with the wisdom of the elements, integrating their teachings into the fabric of life.

The elements remind us that we are not separate from the world but intimately connected to it. They flow through every aspect of existence, from the vastness of the cosmos to the smallest particle within the self. To work with them is to enter into a sacred relationship with the forces that sustain and shape life, to feel their presence in every breath, every step, and every moment.

Through the elemental keys, the mysteries of existence become accessible, not as distant abstractions but as living realities. They open pathways to deeper understanding, guiding the seeker toward balance, harmony, and transformation. In their simplicity and power, the elements hold the essence of creation, inviting all who engage with them to step into the flow of life's eternal emanations.

Chapter 20
Power Centers

Across the surface of the Earth lie locations where energy surges, flows, and converges with extraordinary intensity—places known as power centers. These are not merely geographic points of interest but focal nodes in the planetary web of emanations. Charged with magnetic, telluric, and spiritual forces, power centers hold the potential to transform, heal, and connect those who approach them with reverence and awareness.

Throughout history, humanity has been drawn to these locations, sensing their vitality and resonance. Ancient cultures marked these sites with sacred structures, aligning temples, stone circles, and pyramids with celestial movements and geomagnetic currents. These architectural feats were not arbitrary; they were expressions of a deep understanding of the Earth's energetic matrix, a way to amplify and harmonize the natural flows of energy.

Power centers manifest in various forms: towering mountains, serene lakes, dense forests, or arid deserts. They may be sites of natural beauty or places altered by human intention. What unites them is their role as energetic hubs, where the boundary between the material and the spiritual seems to thin, allowing for heightened perception and profound experiences.

One of the most famous examples is Machu Picchu, the ancient Incan city perched high in the Andes. Beyond its breathtaking vistas, the site is imbued with a palpable energy, a resonance that many visitors describe as deeply grounding and expansive. Similarly, the Great Pyramids of Giza, aligned precisely with celestial coordinates, serve as both physical and energetic monuments, channeling cosmic flows through their geometry.

Stonehenge, another iconic power center, reflects humanity's long-standing relationship with these energies. Its arrangement of massive stones mirrors the cycles of the sun and moon, suggesting its use as both a calendar and a site for rituals that harmonize human activity with celestial rhythms. The magnetic anomalies detected in and around the stones further highlight its role as a conduit for terrestrial and cosmic forces.

The energy of power centers is often associated with ley lines, the invisible pathways of geomagnetic energy that crisscross the Earth. These lines, akin to meridians in the human body, connect sacred sites, forming an intricate network that channels and distributes the planet's energy. Locations where multiple ley lines intersect are particularly potent, serving as vortices of concentrated emanations.

Not all power centers are well-known or easily identified. Many are tucked away in remote regions or hidden in plain sight, accessible only to those who attune themselves to the subtle flows of energy. The process of discovering these places often requires intuition, sensitivity, and an openness to the unseen.

The energy within power centers is not uniform; it varies in quality and intensity. Some locations exude a calming, restorative vibration, ideal for meditation and healing. Others are charged with dynamic, transformative energy, catalyzing profound shifts in perception and consciousness. Understanding the nature of a power center requires attunement to its emanations, a willingness to listen and engage with its unique rhythm.

Engaging with power centers involves more than visiting or observing; it requires active participation. Grounding practices, such as walking barefoot or sitting directly on the earth, foster a direct connection to the site's energy. Meditation and breathwork amplify this connection, allowing the individual to align their own emanations with the flow of the center.

Ceremonial practices further deepen the experience. Offering prayers, lighting candles, or leaving symbolic gifts such as flowers or stones create an exchange of energy, a recognition of the site's significance and a gesture of reciprocity. These rituals, drawn from ancient traditions, honor the power center's role within the larger web of life.

Power centers also serve as spaces for healing and transformation. Many who visit these sites report profound physical, emotional, or spiritual shifts, as though the energy of the location realigns their own vibratory patterns. These transformations are not always gentle; some power centers act as mirrors, reflecting unacknowledged aspects of the self and catalyzing deep inner work.

In addition to individual experiences, power centers play a collective role in balancing the planet's energies. Just as the human body relies on chakras to distribute and harmonize energy, the Earth uses power centers to maintain equilibrium. This connection underscores the importance of preserving and protecting these locations, ensuring that their energy remains accessible for future generations.

The interaction between power centers and celestial events adds another layer of significance. Solstices, equinoxes, and planetary alignments often amplify the energy of these sites, creating moments of heightened resonance. Rituals performed during these times tap into the expanded flow of emanations, aligning human intention with the cosmic rhythm.

Modern technology has begun to explore the scientific dimensions of power centers. Measurements of geomagnetic activity, electromagnetic anomalies, and gravitational shifts provide evidence of their unique energetic properties. While science may not yet fully understand the mechanisms behind these phenomena, it affirms the existence of forces that transcend conventional explanations.

For those unable to visit renowned power centers, the concept of personal sacred spaces offers an alternative. By creating intentional environments—whether in a home, garden, or nearby natural area—individuals can cultivate their own connection to the Earth's energy. These spaces, infused with intention and reverence, act as microcosms of larger power centers, supporting meditation, healing, and spiritual growth.

The journey to a power center is both external and internal. It begins with a physical pilgrimage, a movement through landscapes that reflect the flow of life's emanations. Yet, as the journey unfolds, it becomes clear that the true power of these sites lies within, in the way they awaken and align the energies of the soul.

To engage with power centers is to step into a living relationship with the Earth and the cosmos. It is to recognize the interconnectedness of all things, to feel the currents of energy that flow through the land, the sky, and the self. These places are not static monuments but dynamic expressions of the universal web, pulsing with the vibratory essence of creation.

In their presence, the boundaries between the individual and the infinite blur, revealing a profound truth: that the energy of power centers is not confined to specific locations but flows through all of existence. By attuning to this energy, one aligns with the rhythm of the Earth, stepping into harmony with the vast and timeless emanations that sustain life.

Chapter 21
Dance of the Forces

Movement is the language of energy, a dynamic expression of the emanations that flow through all things. In the rhythm of the tides, the sway of trees, and the pulse of a beating heart, the forces of creation reveal themselves. This eternal dance is not random but guided by patterns of harmony and resonance, where every motion influences the next, creating an endless interplay of form and flow.

Throughout human history, movement has been a way to connect with these forces, to channel and direct energy in alignment with the rhythms of the universe. Sacred dances, rituals, and physical practices serve as bridges between the material and spiritual realms, transforming the body into a vessel for energy to flow freely. The act of moving with intention is not merely an expression but a profound act of creation, shaping the emanations within and around the self.

In many ancient traditions, dance was considered a sacred act. The whirling dervishes of Sufism spin in meditative ecstasy, their movements reflecting the cosmic dance of the universe. Indigenous peoples across the world perform ceremonial dances to invoke spirits, honor the earth, or celebrate the cycles of life. These practices are not performances but spiritual engagements, aligning the participants with the forces they seek to embody.

The relationship between movement and energy is deeply embedded in Eastern practices such as Tai Chi, Qi Gong, and Yoga. These systems emphasize the flow of vital energy—known as *qi*, *prana*, or life force—through the body, using deliberate movements to clear blockages, balance the system, and harmonize with the surrounding environment. Each gesture, no matter how small, becomes a channel for the emanations that sustain life.

Breath, as the subtle partner of movement, plays a crucial role in this dance. The rhythm of inhalation and exhalation mirrors the cycles of expansion and contraction found throughout the cosmos. Practices that synchronize movement with breath amplify the flow of energy, creating a resonance that extends beyond the physical body. This alignment enhances awareness, allowing the practitioner to feel the emanations as they ebb and flow within and around them.

The spiral, a universal symbol of growth and transformation, is often reflected in sacred movements. From the spiral dances of Celtic traditions to the coiling movements of Kundalini Yoga, this pattern represents the natural flow of energy as it ascends and descends, expands and contracts. By moving in spirals, one taps into the cyclical nature of existence, aligning with the rhythms of the earth and the cosmos.

Conscious movement extends beyond structured practices into everyday life. Walking, for instance, becomes a meditative act when performed with awareness, each step grounding the self in the present moment and connecting with the earth's energy. Even mundane gestures carry the potential for alignment when infused with intention, turning the simplest actions into sacred expressions.

Modern somatic practices, such as Feldenkrais and Alexander Technique, explore the relationship between movement, perception, and energy. These approaches focus on subtle adjustments to posture and motion, revealing how small changes can unlock flows of energy and enhance awareness. By cultivating sensitivity to the body's movements, practitioners develop a deeper connection to the emanations that guide and sustain them.

Music and rhythm are natural companions to movement, amplifying its effects and creating resonance. Drumming, in particular, has been used for millennia to induce trance states, where the boundaries between the self and the surrounding energies dissolve. The repetitive beat of a drum mirrors the heartbeat of the earth, guiding participants into alignment with the larger rhythms of existence.

In group settings, movement takes on a collective dimension, amplifying its energetic effects. Circle dances, such as those found in folk traditions or contemporary ecstatic dance practices, create a shared flow of energy that unites participants. The circular formation reflects the interconnected nature of life, where individual emanations merge into a greater whole.

Movement also serves as a tool for healing and transformation. Practices such as dance therapy and somatic release work use motion to access and release stored emotions, trauma, and energetic blockages. By engaging the body in this way, individuals reconnect with their own vitality, restoring balance and harmony to their system.

The interplay of forces in movement is mirrored on a cosmic scale. The planets orbit the sun in elegant arcs, the stars swirl within galaxies, and the universe itself expands and contracts in an eternal rhythm. These celestial dances reflect the same principles found in the movements of the human body, reminding us that we are not separate from the cosmos but participants in its flow.

Practical techniques for engaging with the dance of forces include:

Free Movement: Allowing the body to move spontaneously, without judgment or intention, reveals the natural flow of energy and releases tension.

Rhythmic Walking: Synchronizing steps with breath or a mantra transforms walking into a meditative practice that grounds and aligns.

Energy Circles: Creating spiraling or circular motions with the hands or body activates and harmonizes energy flows, enhancing awareness of emanations.

Engaging with movement also cultivates a deeper understanding of balance. Just as every step requires a moment of instability before finding stability, so too does growth require the willingness to explore new rhythms and patterns. This dance between balance and imbalance mirrors the flow of life itself, where change and adaptation are constant.

The dance of the forces is not confined to human motion; it is present in all aspects of life. The sway of a tree in the wind, the ripple of water in a stream, and the shifting patterns of clouds all reflect the natural flow of energy. By observing these movements, one becomes attuned to the rhythms that guide and sustain existence, deepening the connection to the universal emanations.

To embrace the dance of the forces is to step into alignment with the currents of creation. It is to recognize that every movement, no matter how small, contributes to the greater flow, shaping and reshaping the fabric of reality. Through conscious movement, one becomes a co-creator in the dance of life, attuned to the rhythms of the earth, the cosmos, and the self.

This dance is not a performance but a way of being, a living expression of the emanations that move through all things. By engaging with it fully, one discovers the profound truth of interconnectedness, where every step, gesture, and breath becomes a reflection of the infinite, flowing rhythm of existence.

Chapter 22
The Cosmic Wheel

The cosmos moves in cycles, a vast wheel of time and energy that governs the rhythms of existence. This wheel turns ceaselessly, shaping the flows of emanations that connect the heavens, the earth, and all living beings. The movements of planets, stars, and galaxies form patterns that resonate through every level of reality, from the grandest cosmic cycles to the smallest moments of human experience.

Ancient cultures recognized these celestial rhythms as fundamental to life. They observed the motions of the sun and moon, the changing constellations, and the passage of seasons, weaving these patterns into their understanding of existence. In these cycles, they saw the interplay of forces that sustain the world—a dance of light and shadow, growth and decay, creation and dissolution.

The concept of the cosmic wheel is reflected in countless traditions. The Indian *kala chakra*, or "wheel of time," describes the cyclical nature of existence, encompassing the movements of celestial bodies and the evolution of the soul. The Mayan calendar, with its intricate cycles, reflects a deep understanding of cosmic rhythms and their influence on earthly life. In Norse mythology, Yggdrasil, the World Tree, serves as a cosmic axis, connecting all realms and anchoring the turning wheel of existence.

At the heart of the cosmic wheel lies the cycle of the sun, whose journey defines the rhythms of day and night, solstices and equinoxes, and the changing seasons. The rising sun heralds beginnings and renewal, while its setting marks endings and rest.

The solstices, points of greatest light and darkness, symbolize the balance and interplay of opposing forces. The equinoxes, where day and night are equal, represent moments of harmony and transition.

The moon, with its phases, mirrors these cycles on a more intimate scale. Each phase—from the new moon's darkness to the full moon's radiance—carries its own energetic signature, influencing emotions, intuition, and the flow of emanations. The waxing moon is a time of growth and intention, the full moon a moment of culmination and illumination, and the waning moon a period of release and reflection.

The planets, too, contribute their energies to the cosmic wheel. Their movements, or transits, create ever-changing patterns of influence, shaping the flows of energy that affect individuals and collectives. Astrological traditions interpret these patterns as reflections of cosmic intelligence, offering insights into the connections between the celestial and the earthly.

Beyond the cycles of the sun, moon, and planets lie greater cosmic rhythms, measured in millennia and eons. The precession of the equinoxes, a slow wobble in the Earth's axis, creates a cycle of approximately 26,000 years, dividing time into astrological ages such as the Age of Pisces or the emerging Age of Aquarius. These ages carry distinct energies, influencing the evolution of consciousness and the trajectory of human civilization.

The cosmic wheel is not limited to celestial phenomena; its rhythms are mirrored in the natural world. The growth rings of a tree, the migration patterns of animals, and the tides of the ocean all reflect the cycles of energy that flow through the earth and its inhabitants. Human life, too, follows these patterns, from the cycles of breath and heartbeat to the stages of growth, maturity, and decline.

By aligning with the cosmic wheel, individuals can harmonize their lives with the greater rhythms of existence. This alignment begins with awareness—observing the cycles of the sun, moon, and stars and recognizing their influence on emotions, thoughts, and actions. Simple practices, such as rising with the sun, meditating under the moon, or celebrating the changing seasons, foster a deeper connection to these cycles.

Rituals rooted in the cosmic wheel amplify this connection. Celebrations of solstices and equinoxes, found in traditions worldwide, honor the turning points of the year and their energetic significance. These rituals, whether ancient or modern, align participants with the flows of light and shadow, growth and rest, that shape the natural world.

Astrological practices offer another way to engage with the cosmic wheel. By studying the positions of celestial bodies at a given moment, individuals gain insights into the energies at play and their potential influences. This knowledge can guide decisions, enhance self-awareness, and reveal opportunities for growth and transformation.

The cosmic wheel also invites reflection on the cyclical nature of life itself. Just as the seasons turn from spring to winter, so do human experiences move through cycles of beginning, flourishing, and completion. Recognizing these patterns fosters acceptance and resilience, reminding individuals that every ending holds the seed of a new beginning.

Engaging with the cosmic wheel requires not only observation but also participation. Practices that synchronize the body and spirit with these rhythms deepen the connection to the flows of emanations. Movement practices, such as yoga or dance, performed in harmony with celestial cycles, enhance this alignment. Journaling, intention-setting, and reflection tied to lunar phases or seasonal transitions integrate these energies into daily life.

The cosmic wheel is not static but ever-turning, a reminder that change is the essence of existence. It reflects the interplay of forces—expansion and contraction, light and shadow, order and chaos—that sustain the universe. By embracing these cycles, individuals align with the flow of life, finding balance within its constant movement.

In its turning, the cosmic wheel reveals the interconnectedness of all things. The movements of distant stars influence the earth, just as the rhythms of nature shape the human spirit. These connections are not random but part of a greater harmony, a cosmic dance that weaves together the seen and unseen.

The wheel's turning also carries a message of unity. It reminds us that we are not separate from the cosmos but integral to its flow. Each breath, each step, each thought participates in the cycles of creation and dissolution, contributing to the unfolding patterns of existence.

To live in harmony with the cosmic wheel is to embrace the rhythms of life, to flow with its currents rather than resist them. It is to recognize that every moment—whether of joy or sorrow, growth or rest—is part of a greater whole, a journey guided by the emanations of the universe.

In the turning of the cosmic wheel, one discovers not only the patterns of the heavens but also the depths of the soul. It is a mirror of existence, reflecting the eternal dance of energy and consciousness that sustains all things. To align with it is to step into the flow of creation, becoming a living expression of the infinite cycles that shape the universe.

Chapter 23
Energy in Motion

The body is a vessel of energy, a living conduit through which emanations flow, merge, and transform. Every motion, from the subtle rise and fall of the breath to the sweeping arcs of physical gestures, is a reflection of this dynamic energy in motion. The human form is not merely flesh and bone but a symphony of vibrations, each movement resonating with the unseen currents that shape existence.

Eastern and Western traditions alike have long recognized the power of conscious movement as a means of engaging with these energies. From the flowing forms of Tai Chi to the disciplined postures of Yoga, from the rhythmic steps of sacred dances to the intuitive expressions of modern somatic practices, movement becomes more than a physical act—it becomes a dialogue with the emanations that define life.

In the practice of Tai Chi, the body moves as one with the flow of *qi*, the vital energy that animates all living beings. Slow, deliberate gestures mirror the currents of nature, embodying the principles of balance, harmony, and continuity. This practice is not merely a physical exercise but a meditation in motion, aligning the practitioner's energy with the greater rhythms of the universe. Each step, each shift of weight, channels the flows of *qi*, creating a dance of unity between body, mind, and spirit.

Similarly, Yoga, rooted in ancient Indian tradition, seeks to harmonize *prana*, the life force, through intentional postures and breathwork. The asanas, or physical poses, are not static but dynamic expressions of energy, opening pathways within the body's subtle channels, or nadis. Each pose becomes a gateway, connecting the practitioner to the emanations that flow within and beyond the self. Breath, as the thread that weaves through these movements, amplifies the flow of energy, fostering a profound sense of presence and connection.

In shamanic and indigenous traditions, movement takes the form of ritual dances, where the body becomes a bridge between worlds. The rhythms of drums and the sway of bodies invoke spirits, align with natural forces, and channel healing energies. These dances are not choreographed performances but spontaneous expressions of the soul's interaction with the unseen. They reveal the power of movement to transcend boundaries, creating a space where the physical and spiritual converge.

Somatic practices, such as Feldenkrais or Alexander Technique, focus on subtle adjustments in movement to reveal and release patterns of tension. These approaches view the body as a map of experience, where every habit, emotion, and memory is imprinted. By bringing awareness to movement, these practices unlock stored energy, restoring flow and balance. Each small shift becomes an act of liberation, allowing the body to realign with its natural rhythms.

The interplay of movement and breath lies at the heart of these practices. Breath is not merely a physiological function but a carrier of energy, a conduit through which emanations circulate. Techniques such as pranayama, where breath is controlled and directed, amplify this flow, transforming the act of breathing into a powerful tool for alignment and transformation. The rhythm of breath, when synchronized with movement, creates a resonance that harmonizes the physical, emotional, and energetic dimensions of being.

Energy in motion is not confined to formal practices; it permeates every aspect of life. Walking, for instance, becomes an act of grounding when performed with intention, each step reconnecting the self to the earth's energy. Reaching for an object, bending to pick something up, or even the simple act of sitting down carries the potential for alignment when approached with awareness. In these everyday gestures, the flows of emanations reveal themselves, transforming mundane actions into sacred expressions.

The spiral, a universal symbol of motion and growth, is often reflected in these movements. From the coiling of a snake to the unfurling of a fern, the spiral embodies the natural flow of energy as it expands and contracts, ascends and descends. Practices that incorporate spiral movements—whether in dance, martial arts, or creative expression—tap into this pattern, aligning the body with the rhythms of life.

Group practices amplify the effects of movement, creating shared flows of energy that transcend the individual. In collective settings, such as circle dances or synchronized exercises, participants become part of a greater whole, their movements resonating with one another and with the larger field of energy they create. This collective motion not only strengthens the individual's connection to the flow but also fosters a sense of unity and shared purpose.

Music often accompanies movement, serving as both a catalyst and a guide. The beat of a drum, the melody of a flute, or the resonance of a singing bowl shapes the rhythm and intention of motion, creating a harmonious interplay between sound and energy. These auditory vibrations enhance the flow of emanations, deepening the connection between movement and the unseen forces it engages.

Movement also serves as a tool for healing, unlocking the energy trapped in physical or emotional tension. Practices such as dance therapy or somatic release work use motion to access and transform stored experiences, releasing blockages and restoring balance. By engaging with the body in this way, individuals reconnect with their innate vitality, allowing the flows of emanations to circulate freely once more.

The relationship between movement and energy extends to the natural world. The swaying of trees in the wind, the ripple of water in a stream, and the flight of birds all reflect the dance of energy in motion. By observing and mimicking these natural movements, one aligns with the rhythms of the earth, deepening the connection to its emanations.

Practical techniques for engaging with energy in motion include:

Conscious Walking: Walking with intention, synchronizing steps with breath, transforms this simple act into a meditative practice that grounds and centers.

Free Movement: Allowing the body to move spontaneously, without judgment or planning, reveals the natural flows of energy and fosters emotional release.

Rhythmic Breathwork: Synchronizing breath with gentle motions amplifies the flow of energy, creating a resonance that integrates body and mind.

Energy in motion is not limited by form or structure; it is a living expression of the emanations that flow through all things. Whether through structured practices or spontaneous gestures, movement becomes a way to engage with these forces, to align with their rhythms, and to participate in the eternal dance of creation.

To embrace energy in motion is to recognize the interconnectedness of body, breath, and spirit. It is to feel the currents of life as they move within and around, guiding every action and intention. Through this awareness, movement becomes not only a means of expression but a pathway to alignment, transformation, and connection with the infinite emanations that shape existence.

Chapter 24
The Subtle Language

The universe speaks in a language not bound by words, a communication woven from the threads of vibration, symbols, and energy. This subtle language flows through the fabric of existence, carrying messages from the seen and unseen realms alike. To attune to it is to open the senses beyond their ordinary limits, to hear what cannot be spoken, and to perceive the emanations that guide and shape reality.

This language is the bridge between the material and the spiritual, the external and the internal. It whispers in the rustle of leaves, in the quiet hum of the body's energy fields, and in the spaces between thoughts. It is the voice of intuition, the flash of insight, the sense of knowing that transcends explanation. To listen is not merely to hear but to feel, to resonate with the flows of emanations that move within and around the self.

The subtle language finds expression through symbols, patterns, and archetypes that carry meanings both universal and personal. Across cultures and ages, symbols such as the spiral, the circle, and the tree have conveyed truths about the nature of existence. These shapes are not random; they are echoes of the energetic structures that underlie creation, revealing the hidden currents that flow through all things.

Dreams are a profound expression of the subtle language, a realm where symbols, emotions, and archetypes merge into a tapestry of meaning. In dreams, the ordinary boundaries of time and space dissolve, allowing the subconscious to communicate in its native tongue. A soaring bird may signify freedom or transcendence, while a winding path might represent a journey of self-discovery. Each image, charged with energetic resonance, carries messages from the depths of the soul and beyond.

Intuition is another key to understanding the subtle language. It is the quiet voice that speaks without words, guiding decisions and perceptions with a clarity that defies logic. Intuition arises from the alignment of the self with the flows of emanations, a direct connection to the energy that moves through the web of existence. To trust intuition is to trust the subtle language, to follow its guidance even when it cannot be explained.

Extrasensory perception, such as clairvoyance, telepathy, and psychometry, represents an extension of this attunement. These abilities are not gifts reserved for a few but latent potentials within all beings, accessible through practice and intention. Clairvoyance allows one to see the emanations that shape and surround the physical world, while telepathy bridges the energetic gap between minds. Psychometry, the ability to read the energy of objects, reveals the stories imprinted within their vibrations.

The subtle language also manifests in the natural world, where every element carries its own resonance and message. The wind whispers of change, the water reflects the flow of emotions, and the earth grounds and supports. Animals, too, act as messengers, their behaviors and appearances carrying symbolic meanings that resonate with the observer's inner world. To walk in nature is to enter a dialogue with the universe, where every sound, sight, and sensation becomes part of the conversation.

Symbols and signs often appear in moments of synchronicity, those meaningful coincidences that defy rational explanation. A number repeating itself, an unexpected encounter, or a word overheard at just the right moment carries a message encoded in the subtle language. These occurrences are not random but orchestrated by the flows of energy that connect all things, guiding the individual toward alignment and awareness.

To engage with the subtle language is to cultivate sensitivity to these messages. This begins with awareness—observing the world with an open mind and heart, free from preconceived notions. Meditation and mindfulness quiet the noise of the conscious mind, allowing the subtler voices to be heard. Journaling, especially about dreams, synchronicities, and intuitive insights, creates a record of the dialogue, revealing patterns and themes over time.

Working with the subtle language also involves the practice of interpretation. Symbols and messages carry layers of meaning, both universal and personal. A snake, for example, might represent transformation and healing in one context, while in another, it might signify hidden fears or dangers. The key lies in resonance—what the symbol evokes within the observer's energy field. By tuning into this resonance, the deeper meaning becomes clear.

The subtle language is also a tool for healing, allowing access to the energetic imbalances that underlie physical and emotional challenges. Practices such as energy healing, sound therapy, and chakra alignment translate the subtle language into actions that restore harmony and flow. By listening to the body's signals—the tension in a muscle, the warmth in a palm, the rhythm of the breath—one can identify and release blockages, allowing the emanations to move freely once more.

Art, music, and creative expression are powerful mediums for the subtle language, channels through which energy takes form. A painting, a melody, or a poem speaks directly to the soul, bypassing the filters of logic and reason. These creations carry the essence of their maker's energy, resonating with the observer in ways that words cannot capture. To create is to converse with the universe, to give voice to the inexpressible.

The practice of divination—through tarot, runes, I Ching, or other methods—is another way to engage with the subtle language. These tools do not predict the future but reveal the currents of energy that shape the present, offering insights and guidance. The symbols and patterns that emerge in a reading are mirrors of the seeker's inner world, reflecting the flows of emanations that guide their journey.

To master the subtle language is not to impose meaning but to align with it, to become a listener and interpreter of the universe's infinite expressions. This requires humility, patience, and trust—a willingness to let the messages unfold in their own time and way. The subtle language speaks not to the mind but to the soul, where its truths are felt and known rather than analyzed.

As one deepens their connection to the subtle language, the boundaries between the self and the world begin to dissolve. The messages of the universe are no longer external but arise from within, a reflection of the interconnected flows of energy that unite all things. In this dialogue, the self becomes both speaker and listener, creator and creation, part of the endless conversation that is life itself.

The subtle language is always present, waiting to be heard and understood. It flows in the quiet moments, the unexpected signs, and the inner whispers that guide the way. To attune to it is to step into harmony with the emanations that sustain existence, to feel the pulse of the universe in every breath, every thought, every movement. It is the language of connection, a reminder that all things are one, united in the infinite dance of energy and being.

Chapter 25
Everyday Rituals

Rituals are the threads that weave the sacred into the fabric of everyday life. They are not confined to grand ceremonies or distant traditions; they flow through the ordinary moments, transforming the mundane into the profound. Through intention and presence, everyday rituals create a bridge between the self and the universal emanations, grounding the infinite in the rhythm of daily existence.

Ancient traditions understood that rituals served as both anchors and conduits for energy. A simple gesture—a bow, a chant, the lighting of a candle—became a profound act of alignment, harmonizing the individual with the unseen forces that shape reality. These rituals were not arbitrary but deeply symbolic, echoing the cycles of nature, the movements of the stars, and the flow of life itself.

In the modern world, where the pace of life often disconnects individuals from these flows, everyday rituals offer a way to restore balance and presence. They remind us that every action, no matter how small, carries the potential to align with the emanations of the universe. By approaching daily tasks with intention and reverence, even the most ordinary moments become opportunities for transformation.

The morning, as the threshold between night and day, is a powerful time for ritual. Rising with the sun, breathing deeply, and offering gratitude for the new day attunes the self to the cycles of light and renewal. Practices such as journaling, meditation, or stretching set the tone for the hours ahead, creating a flow of energy that supports clarity and purpose.

The act of preparing and consuming food is another natural ritual. In many cultures, meals are accompanied by blessings or prayers, acknowledging the energy of the earth, the hands that harvested and prepared the food, and the nourishment it provides. Eating mindfully, savoring each bite, transforms a routine meal into a moment of connection with the emanations that sustain life.

Rituals of cleansing, whether through bathing, smudging with herbs, or simply washing one's hands, hold symbolic and energetic significance. Water, as a conductor of energy, carries away stagnation and restores flow, both physically and spiritually. Adding intention to these acts—such as visualizing impurities dissolving or repeating affirmations—enhances their transformative power.

Even the act of walking can become a ritual. With each step, one connects to the energy of the earth, grounding the self in its rhythms. By walking with awareness, focusing on breath and sensation, one enters a meditative state, aligning with the flow of emanations within and around them. This practice, often referred to as walking meditation, turns an ordinary activity into a sacred journey.

Rituals of transition—such as lighting a candle at the end of the workday, pausing to reflect before a meal, or setting intentions before sleep—mark the boundaries between one phase and the next. These acts create space for reflection and renewal, allowing energy to flow smoothly through the cycles of life.

The spaces we inhabit also hold energy, and tending to these spaces is a form of ritual. Decluttering, arranging objects with intention, and incorporating elements such as plants, crystals, or sacred symbols infuse the environment with harmony and vitality. Practices such as smudging with sage or ringing a bell clear stagnant energy, creating a space where emanations can move freely.

For many, rituals are deeply personal, shaped by individual needs, beliefs, and experiences. A cup of tea sipped in quiet reflection, a journal entry written by candlelight, or a moment of stillness under the night sky can hold as much power as the grandest ceremony. What matters is not the form but the intention—the awareness that each act is a dialogue with the universe.

Group rituals, whether shared within families, communities, or spiritual circles, amplify this connection. A communal meal, a circle of prayer, or a collective meditation creates a shared flow of energy that strengthens bonds and aligns intentions. These gatherings are not only acts of connection but also opportunities to contribute to the larger field of collective emanations, offering healing and harmony to the world.

Rituals aligned with natural cycles deepen this resonance. Honoring the phases of the moon, the turning of the seasons, or the solstices and equinoxes connects the self to the rhythms of the cosmos. These rituals remind us that we are not separate from nature but part of its infinite dance, subject to the same flows of creation and transformation.

For those seeking to cultivate everyday rituals, simplicity is key. A single moment of gratitude, a quiet breath before beginning a task, or a gesture of kindness toward oneself or another can hold profound significance. These acts do not require elaborate preparation or special tools; they only require presence and intention.

Practical ideas for everyday rituals include:

Morning Alignment: Begin the day with a moment of stillness, a deep breath, and an intention for the hours ahead.

Sacred Eating: Pause before meals to express gratitude, acknowledging the energy and effort that brought the food to the table.

Evening Reflection: Before sleep, reflect on the day's experiences, releasing what no longer serves and expressing gratitude for moments of growth and connection.

Environmental Care: Tend to your space with awareness, arranging objects mindfully and incorporating elements that resonate with your energy.

These small acts, repeated daily, create a foundation of alignment and presence. They weave the sacred into the ordinary, transforming the patterns of life into a continuous flow of connection and meaning.

Everyday rituals also offer a path through challenges and transitions. In times of uncertainty or change, these practices provide stability and grounding, anchoring the self in the flow of emanations. They remind us that even in the midst of chaos, there is a rhythm and a purpose to every moment.

As one cultivates these rituals, the boundary between the sacred and the mundane begins to dissolve. Each action, each breath, becomes an expression of the universal energy that flows through all things. Life itself becomes a ritual, a dance of connection and creation, where every moment holds the potential for alignment and transformation.

Through everyday rituals, the infinite enters the finite, and the ordinary becomes extraordinary. They remind us that the sacred is not something distant or separate but something we carry within, woven into the fabric of our lives. By honoring these practices, we step into harmony with the emanations that guide and sustain existence, creating a life that is both grounded and transcendent.

Chapter 26
Hidden Guardians

The universe is alive with presences, forces, and entities that dwell in the spaces between the visible and the unseen. These hidden guardians, often described in spiritual and mystical traditions, do not merely exist in isolation but serve as stewards of balance and harmony within the energetic realms. Their roles are as varied as their forms, ranging from protectors and guides to regulators of energy flows, bridging the dimensions of existence in ways that remain largely mysterious to human perception.

Across cultures and traditions, these beings have been revered, invoked, and depicted in countless ways. In ancient Greece, the daimon was seen as a personal spirit guide, an intermediary between the human and the divine. In Vedic traditions, the devas and asuras represent forces of light and shadow, maintaining the dynamic balance of creation. Indigenous peoples speak of spirit animals or nature guardians, beings intricately tied to the elements, landscapes, and cycles of life.

While their forms and names differ, the essence of these hidden guardians remains consistent: they are expressions of the universal emanations, embodiments of the energies that shape and sustain existence. Their presence can be subtle, felt as a whisper of intuition, a sudden insight, or an unexplainable sense of protection. At other times, they manifest vividly, appearing in dreams, visions, or moments of deep spiritual connection.

Among the most well-known hidden guardians are the angels, described in various religious and mystical texts as messengers of divine will. Angels are often seen as beings of light, their vibrational frequency so high that they exist beyond the physical plane. They act as intermediaries between the human and the celestial, offering guidance, comfort, and protection. In Kabbalistic tradition, the angelic hierarchy reflects the structure of emanations, with each angel embodying specific aspects of divine energy.

Elemental beings, another form of hidden guardian, are said to dwell within the forces of nature. The sylphs of air, undines of water, salamanders of fire, and gnomes of earth represent the energetic essence of their respective elements. These beings are not separate from the elements they embody but are integral to their flow, maintaining balance and harmony within the natural world.

The idea of ancestral guardians is prevalent in many cultures. These spirits, connected through bloodlines or spiritual lineage, watch over the living, offering wisdom and protection. In African and Afro-Caribbean traditions, ancestor veneration forms the foundation of spiritual practice, acknowledging the continuing presence and influence of those who have passed. These guardians act as bridges between the physical world and the realms of spirit, guiding their descendants through the flows of life.

Hidden guardians are not limited to benevolent forces; traditions also speak of entities that challenge, test, or obstruct. These beings, often described as shadows or tricksters, serve an essential purpose in the grand design. They reveal imbalances, expose hidden fears, and catalyze growth through their challenges. In shamanic practices, these forces are not seen as enemies but as teachers, their presence prompting deeper self-awareness and transformation.

To connect with hidden guardians requires attunement to the subtle realms. This begins with cultivating stillness and presence, allowing the senses to expand beyond the physical. Meditation, dreamwork, and energy practices create pathways for perceiving and engaging with these beings. Symbols, rituals, and invocations further enhance this connection, inviting their presence into the conscious experience.

Discernment is crucial in these interactions. Not all energies are aligned with harmony or growth, and developing the ability to sense the resonance of a presence is essential. Practices such as grounding, energetic shielding, and calling on known protective forces, such as archangels or personal guides, create a safe and stable foundation for exploration.

Hidden guardians often communicate through signs, symbols, and synchronicities. A feather appearing unexpectedly, a sudden shift in the wind, or an animal crossing one's path at a meaningful moment can carry messages from these beings. Dreams, too, serve as a powerful medium for their guidance, offering insights and clarity through imagery and emotion.

While some hidden guardians are associated with specific traditions or cosmologies, others are deeply personal, unique to the individual's journey. These personal guardians may not fit into established archetypes but reveal themselves through repeated encounters, intuitive knowing, or transformative experiences. Their presence is a reminder of the intimate connection between the self and the greater web of emanations.

In group settings, the presence of hidden guardians often becomes more pronounced. Ceremonies, rituals, and collective meditations create an amplified energetic field, making it easier to perceive and engage with these beings. Many spiritual traditions incorporate invocations or offerings to guardians at the beginning of such gatherings, acknowledging their role in holding space and guiding the group's energy.

The relationship with hidden guardians is reciprocal. While they offer guidance, protection, and insight, they also thrive on acknowledgment and respect. Acts of gratitude, such as offering a prayer, lighting a candle, or simply expressing thanks, strengthen the bond between the individual and these beings. This exchange of energy reinforces the alignment with the flows of emanations, fostering harmony and mutual growth.

Hidden guardians also play a collective role, maintaining balance within the larger energetic systems of the planet and the cosmos. Ley lines, sacred sites, and natural phenomena are often described as places where their presence is particularly strong. These beings are seen as caretakers of these energetic nodes, ensuring the continued flow and alignment of energy through the interconnected web of life.

For those seeking to deepen their connection with hidden guardians, practical steps include:

Meditative Invitations: Entering a state of stillness and silently inviting guidance, being open to subtle impressions or sensations.

Symbolic Offerings: Placing meaningful objects, such as stones, flowers, or written intentions, in a sacred space to honor their presence.

Dream Journaling: Recording dreams upon waking to identify recurring symbols or themes that may signify a guardian's message.

Nature Connection: Spending time in natural settings, observing the elements and their movements, and listening for the quiet presence of elemental beings.

Engaging with hidden guardians is not about control or command but about partnership and alignment. These beings, like the flows of emanations they embody, cannot be forced or manipulated. Instead, they respond to sincerity, respect, and a willingness to learn and grow.

The existence of hidden guardians serves as a reminder of the universe's infinite layers and dimensions, of the intricate networks of energy that sustain and shape reality. Their presence, whether felt as a whisper in the wind or a profound spiritual encounter, invites us to look beyond the surface of life, to explore the unseen forces that guide and protect us.

Through these relationships, the boundaries of perception expand, revealing the depth and richness of existence. Hidden guardians are not separate from us; they are reflections of the energies that flow through all things, mirrors of the infinite interconnectedness that binds the self to the cosmos. To engage with them is to step into a deeper awareness of the universal emanations, to walk in partnership with the unseen, and to honor the sacred mystery of life itself.

Chapter 27
Energetic Balance

The universe thrives on balance, an intricate dance of forces that sustain creation and allow the flows of energy to remain in harmony. Within this grand equilibrium, the human being exists as a microcosm of the greater whole, reflecting the universal interplay of light and shadow, stillness and motion, expansion and contraction. Energetic balance, therefore, is not merely a state of inner harmony but a dynamic alignment with the emanations that move through the cosmos.

In ancient traditions, balance was seen as the foundation of health and well-being, extending beyond the physical to encompass the emotional, mental, and spiritual realms. The Chinese concept of yin and yang encapsulates this principle, illustrating how seemingly opposing forces are interdependent and complementary. Similarly, the Ayurvedic system emphasizes the balance of the three doshas—vata, pitta, and kapha—as essential to maintaining vitality and harmony.

Energetic balance begins with awareness, the ability to perceive the flows of energy within and around the self. These flows, while invisible to the eye, can be felt through subtle sensations, emotions, and states of mind. A sense of vitality and ease often indicates alignment, while feelings of stagnation, agitation, or depletion suggest imbalance. This sensitivity, cultivated through practices such as meditation and mindfulness, allows one to identify and address disruptions before they manifest as physical or emotional challenges.

The causes of energetic imbalance are as varied as life itself. External factors, such as stress, environmental toxins, or chaotic surroundings, can disrupt the natural flow of energy. Internal factors, including unresolved emotions, limiting beliefs, or physical illness, further contribute to disharmony. These imbalances often manifest as blockages or leaks within the energy field, impeding the free movement of emanations.

Restoring energetic balance requires a holistic approach, addressing not only the symptoms but also the underlying causes. Practices that engage the body, mind, and spirit in unison are particularly effective, creating a ripple effect that restores harmony across all levels of being.

Breathwork serves as a powerful tool for balancing energy. The breath is the bridge between the physical and subtle bodies, a rhythm that connects the inner and outer worlds. Techniques such as alternate nostril breathing (Nadi Shodhana) calm the mind and harmonize the energy channels, or nadis, within the subtle body. Deep, conscious breathing revitalizes the system, releasing tension and restoring the natural flow of emanations.

Movement, too, plays a vital role in maintaining balance. Practices such as Yoga, Tai Chi, and Qi Gong align the body with the rhythms of energy, opening pathways and dissolving stagnation. These movements, performed with awareness, create a flow that extends beyond the physical, harmonizing the emotional and spiritual dimensions. Even simple actions, such as stretching, walking, or swaying with intention, activate the body's natural ability to restore balance.

Energetic cleansing is another essential practice. Just as the body requires hygiene, the energy field benefits from regular clearing to release accumulated negativity or stagnation. Smudging with sage, bathing with salt water, or using sound tools such as bells or singing bowls effectively clear the field, creating space for fresh energy to circulate. Visualization techniques, such as imagining a golden light washing over the body, further enhance this process.

Grounding, the act of reconnecting with the earth's energy, stabilizes the energy field and restores balance. Walking barefoot on the ground, sitting under a tree, or simply placing one's hands on the earth creates an exchange of energy that calms the mind and strengthens the connection to the present moment. Grounding is particularly effective for those who feel scattered, overwhelmed, or disconnected.

Emotional balance is deeply intertwined with energetic harmony. Emotions are currents of energy, and their suppression or overexpression can create disruptions within the field. Practices such as journaling, therapy, or heart-centered meditation help to process and release emotions, allowing their energy to flow freely. Compassion, both for oneself and others, transforms dense or stagnant emotions into lighter, more harmonious vibrations.

The energy centers, or chakras, serve as focal points for balance within the subtle body. Each chakra governs specific aspects of being, from survival and creativity to love, communication, and spiritual connection. When a chakra is blocked or overactive, the flow of energy becomes disrupted, affecting the corresponding physical, emotional, or mental domains. Chakra healing practices, such as visualization, sound therapy, or working with crystals, restore alignment, allowing energy to flow smoothly through the system.

The environment also plays a significant role in energetic balance. Spaces that are cluttered, chaotic, or filled with negative energy can amplify imbalance. Creating a harmonious environment—through organization, intentional decor, or the inclusion of natural elements such as plants or sunlight—supports the flow of energy. Regularly clearing and consecrating the space, using techniques such as smudging or ringing bells, ensures that it remains a sanctuary of balance.

Diet and hydration influence energy in profound ways. Foods carry their own energetic vibrations, and consuming a diet rich in fresh, whole, and nourishing ingredients enhances vitality. Hydration is equally important, as water acts as a conductor of energy, supporting the flow of emanations within the body.

Offering gratitude before meals aligns the act of nourishment with the flow of energy, transforming it into a ritual of balance.

Protective practices help maintain energetic balance amidst challenging environments or interactions. Visualizing a shield of light surrounding the body creates a boundary that filters external energies while allowing positive emanations to flow freely. Affirmations, such as "I am protected and balanced," reinforce this boundary, fostering a sense of stability and strength.

Energetic balance extends beyond the individual to encompass relationships and communities. Harmonizing the energy within interactions fosters understanding, compassion, and connection, creating a ripple effect that benefits all involved. Practices such as group meditations, collective rituals, or simply approaching interactions with mindfulness contribute to this shared balance.

Life's rhythms, with their inevitable highs and lows, call for a dynamic approach to balance. Rather than striving for a static state, energetic harmony embraces the ebb and flow of existence, adjusting to each moment with presence and adaptability. This flexibility reflects the nature of balance itself—a constant interplay of forces, each supporting and complementing the other.

Engaging with balance requires awareness, intention, and action. By attuning to the flows of energy and responding to their shifts, one becomes a co-creator in the dance of harmony. The journey toward balance is not a destination but an ongoing process, a living relationship with the emanations that sustain life.

To cultivate energetic balance is to align with the rhythms of the universe, to flow with its currents rather than resist them. It is to recognize that harmony is not the absence of challenge but the presence of alignment—a state where every force, whether light or shadow, finds its rightful place within the whole. Through this alignment, the self becomes a reflection of the cosmos, a vessel through which the infinite dance of balance unfolds.

Chapter 28
Cosmic Geometry

Throughout the universe, geometry reveals itself as the silent architect of creation. From the spiraling arms of galaxies to the intricate patterns of a snowflake, the language of form speaks to an underlying order, a profound intelligence shaping the emanations that flow through all things. This is cosmic geometry—the sacred interplay of shapes, patterns, and proportions that govern existence on every scale.

At the heart of cosmic geometry lies the principle that energy organizes itself through form. Each geometric structure is an expression of vibratory frequencies, the visible manifestation of the unseen. These forms are not static; they are dynamic, pulsing with the energy of creation, reflecting the harmony that sustains the universe.

Ancient cultures understood the power of geometric patterns, embedding them within their sacred art, architecture, and spiritual practices. The Egyptians, for instance, constructed the pyramids using precise proportions that mirrored celestial alignments and vibrational harmony. The Flower of Life, a symbol found in temples across the world, illustrates the interconnectedness of all things through overlapping circles, each representing a node in the infinite web of emanations.

One of the most universal geometric patterns is the spiral, a form that appears in galaxies, hurricanes, seashells, and the structure of DNA. The spiral embodies the flow of energy as it expands and contracts, mirroring the cycles of growth and transformation that define existence. To follow the spiral is to move in harmony with the rhythms of creation, aligning with the dynamic currents that shape life.

The golden ratio, or *phi*, is another cornerstone of cosmic geometry. This proportion, approximately 1.618, appears in the growth patterns of plants, the proportions of the human body, and even the structure of galaxies. The golden ratio reflects balance and harmony, guiding the organization of matter and energy into forms that resonate with the flows of emanations.

The Platonic solids—five geometric shapes where each face is identical—hold particular significance in cosmic geometry. These forms, named after the philosopher Plato, are seen as the building blocks of the universe, corresponding to the classical elements: earth (cube), air (octahedron), fire (tetrahedron), water (icosahedron), and ether (dodecahedron). Each shape embodies specific energetic qualities, serving as a bridge between the material and spiritual realms.

Sacred geometry extends beyond natural forms into human creation. Mandalas, intricate geometric designs used in meditation and ritual, reflect the structure of the cosmos and the inner workings of the mind. The symmetry and balance of a mandala guide the observer into a state of alignment, harmonizing the emanations within and around them. Similarly, yantras, geometric diagrams used in Hindu and Tantric traditions, serve as tools for focusing energy and consciousness, channeling the flows of *prana* toward spiritual awakening.

The power of cosmic geometry lies not only in its forms but in its ability to resonate with the soul. To gaze upon a geometric pattern is to feel its vibration, to align with its harmony. This resonance is not limited to sight; it extends to sound, where frequencies create geometric shapes in a phenomenon known as cymatics. When sand or water is subjected to specific vibrations, it forms intricate patterns, revealing the connection between sound and form.

Architectural spaces designed with sacred geometry amplify this resonance, creating environments that enhance energy flow and spiritual connection. Gothic cathedrals, with their soaring arches and intricate rose windows, reflect these principles, their forms channeling light and sound in ways that inspire awe and alignment. Modern spaces, too, can incorporate cosmic geometry through intentional design, creating homes, gardens, and workplaces that resonate with balance and harmony.

Working with cosmic geometry involves more than observation; it requires participation. By creating or engaging with geometric forms, one aligns with their vibratory essence, inviting their energy into the self. Drawing a mandala, constructing a geometric sculpture, or meditating with a yantra becomes an act of connection, a dialogue with the universal patterns that shape existence.

Practical exercises for engaging with cosmic geometry include:

Meditation on Forms: Gazing at a geometric pattern, such as the Flower of Life or a mandala, while focusing on its symmetry and flow.

Drawing Sacred Shapes: Recreating geometric designs by hand, allowing the process to become a meditative practice that aligns the mind and body.

Sound and Cymatics: Experimenting with sound frequencies to create visible patterns in water or sand, observing the relationship between vibration and form.

Cosmic geometry also invites exploration through movement. Practices such as spiral dancing, where participants move in patterns that mimic the flow of energy, create a physical alignment with geometric principles. Similarly, yoga poses that emphasize balance, symmetry, and circular motion reflect these patterns within the body, aligning the physical and energetic fields.

The connection between cosmic geometry and the natural world is profound. Each leaf, petal, and branch grows according to these principles, revealing the universe's inherent order. Observing these patterns in nature—whether in the symmetry of a flower, the spiral of a seashell, or the fractal branching of a tree—deepens the understanding of geometry as a living force.

As one engages with cosmic geometry, the perception of the universe begins to shift. The seemingly chaotic becomes ordered, the fragmented becomes whole. Each shape, each pattern, is revealed as a reflection of the infinite emanations that flow through all things. This awareness fosters a sense of connection, a recognition that the self is not separate from the cosmos but a part of its intricate design.

Cosmic geometry is not merely a study of shapes but a path to alignment and awakening. It is a reminder that the universe is built on harmony, that every form carries within it the essence of creation. By attuning to these forms, one steps into the flow of the universal emanations, aligning with the patterns that sustain life.

In the dance of shapes and vibrations, cosmic geometry reveals the profound truth of existence: that everything is connected, bound by the same harmonies that move through the stars, the earth, and the soul. Through this alignment, the self becomes a living expression of the sacred patterns, a vessel for the infinite energy that shapes the universe.

Chapter 29
Vital Breath

The breath is the rhythm of life, a continuous exchange between the self and the universe. With each inhalation, the body draws in the essence of creation; with each exhalation, it releases and renews. This cycle is more than a physical necessity—it is a bridge between the visible and the invisible, a conduit for the emanations that sustain existence. To breathe is to participate in the flow of life itself, to align with the forces that shape and move through the cosmos.

Ancient traditions understood the profound significance of breath, recognizing it as the carrier of vital energy. In the Vedic traditions of India, breath is called *prana*, the life force that flows through all beings. Chinese philosophy names this energy *qi*, circulating through the meridians and sustaining the body and spirit. In the Greco-Roman world, it was known as *pneuma* or *spiritus*, connecting the material and the divine. Across cultures, breath is more than air; it is the essence of life, the thread that ties the physical to the spiritual.

The act of breathing, though automatic, holds untapped potential. When approached with awareness and intention, breath transforms into a powerful tool for alignment, healing, and transformation. Each breath becomes a dialogue with the universe, a way to harmonize with the flows of emanations that move within and beyond the self.

Breath's relationship with energy begins with its rhythm. The length, depth, and speed of each breath influence the flow of energy, affecting the body, mind, and spirit. Shallow, rapid breaths create tension and fragmentation, while deep, slow breaths foster relaxation, clarity, and connection. By consciously altering the rhythm of the breath, one can shift their energetic state, moving from chaos to calm, from depletion to vitality.

In many spiritual practices, the control of breath, or pranayama, is central to the cultivation of energy. Techniques such as alternate nostril breathing (Nadi Shodhana) balance the left and right channels of energy, harmonizing the dual forces of the body and mind. Kapalabhati, or "skull-shining breath," invigorates the system, clearing stagnation and awakening dormant energy. Each practice, though simple, carries profound effects, unlocking the flows of *prana* and creating alignment with the universal currents.

Breath also serves as a bridge to altered states of consciousness. Practices such as holotropic breathing, developed for deep inner exploration, use rhythmic, intensified breathing to access realms beyond the ordinary mind. These techniques dissolve the boundaries of the self, allowing the practitioner to merge with the emanations of the cosmos, to touch the infinite within.

The connection between breath and emotion is equally profound. Each emotion carries its own rhythm of breath: anger might manifest as short, jagged breaths, while sadness slows and deepens the exhale. By consciously shifting the breath, one can transform emotional states, releasing tension or fostering resilience. This interplay highlights breath as both a mirror and a tool for energetic harmony.

In movement practices, the synchronization of breath and motion amplifies the flow of energy. In Yoga, each pose (asana) is guided by the breath, creating a seamless connection between the body's movements and the inner currents of energy. Tai Chi and Qi Gong similarly integrate breath with motion, each gesture flowing with the rhythm of inhalation and exhalation. This alignment transforms physical activity into a moving meditation, harmonizing the self with the emanations of life.

Breath extends beyond the individual, acting as a shared rhythm that unites groups and communities. In collective practices, such as group meditation or chanting, the synchronization of breath creates a powerful field of energy, amplifying its effects. This shared rhythm reflects the interconnectedness of all beings, reminding participants that they are part of a greater whole.

The physical benefits of breath are well-documented, yet they are only the beginning. Deep, intentional breathing oxygenates the body, calms the nervous system, and enhances focus, but its effects extend to the subtle realms as well. Through breath, one can access and influence the energy centers of the body, the chakras, clearing blockages and restoring balance. Each breath becomes a flow of light, illuminating and energizing the pathways within.

Breath also connects the self to the natural world. The rhythm of the breath mirrors the cycles of the earth—the rise and fall of waves, the sway of trees in the wind, the rhythm of the tides. By attuning the breath to these natural patterns, one deepens their connection to the emanations of the earth, aligning their energy with the larger rhythms of existence.

Practical techniques for working with breath include:

Deep Diaphragmatic Breathing: Focusing on expanding the abdomen with each inhale and softening it with each exhale, calming the nervous system and grounding energy.

Box Breathing: Inhaling, holding, exhaling, and holding the breath for equal counts (e.g., four counts each) to create a sense of stability and focus.

Ocean Breath (Ujjayi): Gently constricting the throat while breathing to create a soft, wave-like sound, fostering presence and concentration.

In moments of chaos or uncertainty, returning to the breath provides an anchor. A single conscious inhale and exhale is enough to create a pause, a moment of clarity amidst the noise. This simplicity is the breath's greatest gift: it is always available, always flowing, a constant reminder of the life force that sustains all things.

The breath also carries a spiritual dimension, acting as a bridge between the self and the divine. Many traditions incorporate breath in prayer or meditation, using it as a way to connect with higher realms. The Sufi practice of *zikr*, for example, combines breath with repetitive chanting, aligning the practitioner with the sacred emanations of the divine.

Through breath, one learns to listen—to the body, the emotions, the subtle energies within. Each breath becomes a message, a guide, a way to attune to the flows of life. This awareness transforms the act of breathing from a subconscious function into a conscious act of creation, a way to align with the emanations of the universe.

Vital breath is the essence of existence, the rhythm of life that connects all beings. It flows through the individual, the collective, and the cosmos, carrying the energy that sustains and transforms. To work with breath is to work with the core of life itself, to step into the flow of creation, and to align with the infinite currents that shape reality.

Through the breath, one discovers the profound truth of interconnectedness, that each inhale and exhale is part of a greater cycle, a shared rhythm that unites all things. By honoring this flow, by breathing with intention and awareness, one becomes a vessel for the emanations of life, a living expression of the infinite breath that moves through the cosmos.

Chapter 30
Transformative Flames

Fire is the ancient force of transformation, a luminous presence that consumes, purifies, and renews. It is both a symbol and a reality, the alchemical agent that turns one form into another. From the flickering candle to the roaring inferno, fire reflects the ceaseless movement of energy, the emanations of life in their most dynamic and transformative state.

Throughout history, fire has been revered as sacred, a bridge between the physical and the spiritual. In the Vedic traditions of India, the fire altar—*agni*—served as the focal point of ritual, connecting the human to the divine. In Zoroastrianism, the eternal flame symbolized the purity of spirit and the presence of the divine in the material world. In countless cultures, fire ceremonies were performed to invoke protection, offer gratitude, and catalyze transformation, reflecting humanity's deep understanding of fire as a force of energetic alignment.

The essence of fire lies in its ability to transmute. It consumes the old, clearing space for the new. This principle is not limited to the physical world; it extends to the emotional, mental, and spiritual realms. Fire is the energy of release, of letting go of what no longer serves, transforming dense or stagnant emanations into light and vitality.

Within the self, the transformative flames reside as an inner fire. This fire is not physical but energetic, a vital force that fuels growth, creativity, and spiritual awakening. In Yogic tradition, this inner fire is called *tapas*, the heat of discipline and transformation. It is stoked through practices that challenge and refine, burning away impurities and illuminating the path toward alignment with the flows of life.

The solar plexus chakra, or *Manipura*, is often associated with this inner flame. Located at the core of the body, it is the center of willpower, confidence, and transformation. When this chakra is balanced, the inner fire burns brightly, empowering the individual to act with clarity and purpose. When blocked or overactive, the flame dims or flares uncontrollably, leading to stagnation or imbalance.

Engaging with fire as a transformative force begins with recognizing its dual nature. Fire can nurture and destroy, enlighten and consume. It is neither inherently benevolent nor malevolent; its effects depend on intention and alignment. To work with fire is to harness its energy with respect and awareness, using it as a tool for growth and renewal.

Rituals involving fire tap into its profound transformative power. Lighting a candle with intention transforms a simple act into a sacred practice, the flame becoming a symbol of focus and clarity. Writing fears, regrets, or limiting beliefs on paper and burning them releases their energy, creating space for new possibilities. In these rituals, the flame acts as an intermediary, carrying the emanations of intention into the realms of transformation.

The alchemical nature of fire is also reflected in the physical process of combustion. Fire breaks bonds, releasing energy stored within matter. On a spiritual level, this mirrors the breaking of old patterns, the dissolution of attachments, and the liberation of the self from constraints. Fire teaches that transformation is not a gentle process but a dynamic one, requiring courage and surrender to its purifying heat.

The transformative flames are not confined to rituals or inner work; they are present in every aspect of life. Moments of challenge, change, and upheaval are manifestations of this energy, opportunities for growth through the fires of experience. These moments, while often uncomfortable, are invitations to release, to transform, and to emerge renewed.

Fire also reveals the interconnectedness of destruction and creation. In nature, wildfires clear forests of deadwood, making way for new growth. Volcanic eruptions, though destructive, create fertile land. This principle extends to the personal and collective realms, where the dissolution of the old—though painful—paves the way for renewal and evolution.

In movement practices, the energy of fire is invoked through dynamic, rhythmic motions that generate heat and awaken the inner flame. Practices such as Kundalini Yoga or ecstatic dance channel this energy, breaking through stagnation and activating transformation. These movements, performed with intention, align the physical and energetic bodies with the emanations of fire, creating a flow of vitality and renewal.

Sound also carries the essence of fire. Chanting mantras, such as the Sanskrit *Om Agnaye Namaha* (salutation to the fire deity Agni), resonates with the transformative flames, amplifying their energy. Drumming, with its rhythmic intensity, invokes the primal force of fire, its vibrations igniting the inner and outer flows of transformation.

The transformative flames are not limited to the individual; they extend to the collective. Societies, like individuals, undergo cycles of destruction and renewal, the fires of change burning away outdated structures and beliefs. These moments of collective transformation, though often turbulent, carry the potential for profound growth and alignment with the greater emanations of life.

Working with the transformative flames requires trust and intention. It is a process of surrendering to the heat of change, allowing the old to dissolve so that the new can emerge. This trust is cultivated through practices that align the self with fire's energy, creating a sense of stability amidst its dynamic flow.

Practical techniques for engaging with transformative flames include:

Candle Meditation: Focusing on the flame of a candle, allowing its light to guide the mind into stillness and clarity.

Fire Writing: Writing what needs to be released on paper and burning it, visualizing the flames transforming the energy into light.

Breath of Fire: A rapid, rhythmic breath practice that generates inner heat, awakening the transformative energy within.

Fire also teaches the importance of balance. Just as a fire needs the right conditions to burn steadily—neither smothered nor uncontrolled—the inner and outer flames require care and awareness. Overexertion or neglect disrupts the flow, while mindful tending creates a steady, transformative force.

The transformative flames are not only a force of destruction but also a beacon of creation. They illuminate the path forward, casting light on what is possible. To engage with this energy is to step into the flow of transformation, to become an active participant in the cycles of renewal that shape existence.

Through fire, one learns to embrace change, to release fear and resistance, and to align with the dynamic currents of life. The flames become a mirror of the self, reflecting both the potential for growth and the courage required to pursue it.

In the dance of destruction and creation, the transformative flames reveal the essence of existence: that life is ever-changing, ever-renewing, and infinitely connected. By working with this energy, one aligns with the universal emanations, becoming a vessel for the light and warmth of transformation, a living flame in the infinite fire of the cosmos.

Chapter 31
Silent Wisdom

Amid the constant hum of existence, silence emerges as the most profound teacher. It is within silence that the subtlest emanations reveal themselves, where the vast currents of life can be felt, understood, and aligned with. To embrace silence is to listen to the universe itself, to open the soul to the wisdom that lies beyond words.

In many ancient traditions, silence was revered not as an absence but as a presence—an active state of being that bridges the mundane and the sacred. The mystics of the East sat in deep stillness, their breaths synchronized with the rhythms of nature, allowing them to dissolve into the infinite. The Desert Fathers of early Christianity retreated into vast, unbroken quiet, finding in silence the voice of the divine. Across cultures, silence was seen as the space where the soul could commune with the emanations that sustain existence.

Silence possesses layers, each deeper than the last. The outermost is the physical stillness, the absence of external noise. Beneath this lies the silence of the mind, a tranquil state where thoughts lose their urgency and settle like leaves on a calm pond. Deeper still is the silence of the heart, a profound stillness where emotions align with the flow of life, dissolving into a state of unity. At its core lies the silence of being, an experience of pure presence where the self merges with the universal.

The path to silence begins with awareness. In a world of constant motion and sound, silence can feel foreign, even uncomfortable. Yet, it is precisely in this discomfort that transformation begins. To sit in silence is to confront the inner noise, to witness the restlessness of the mind and the unspoken currents of the heart. Through this witnessing, silence gradually expands, revealing itself not as emptiness but as fullness—a field of infinite potential.

Practices that cultivate silence are tools for entering this sacred state. Meditation, in its essence, is a journey into silence. Whether through focusing on the breath, repeating a mantra, or simply observing the flow of thoughts, meditation quiets the outer layers of being, allowing the deeper silence to emerge. Even a few moments of stillness each day can create ripples of peace, aligning the self with the emanations of life.

The silence of nature holds a unique power, offering a direct connection to the flows of energy. The rustle of leaves, the rhythm of waves, the stillness of a mountain—these sounds are not interruptions but invitations to attune to the natural silence that pervades all things. Walking in nature without speaking or listening to artificial sounds opens the senses, allowing the emanations of the earth to flow freely into the self.

Silence is also a space for reflection, a mirror where the soul can see itself clearly. In the absence of distraction, truths long hidden come to light. This clarity is not always comfortable; silence often reveals what we seek to avoid. Yet, in this revelation lies the key to transformation. By facing the shadows that arise in silence, one can integrate them, transforming their dense energies into light.

The relationship between silence and sound is deeply intertwined. Sound emerges from silence and returns to it, each note carrying the essence of the stillness from which it arose. Practices such as chanting or toning use sound as a tool to deepen silence, creating vibrations that align the energy field before dissolving into quiet. This interplay reflects the cycles of life itself, the dance of creation and dissolution that underlies all things.

In relationships, silence can be a powerful tool for connection. To sit in quiet companionship with another, without the need for words, creates a space where the deeper emanations of presence can be felt. This shared silence fosters understanding and intimacy, transcending the limitations of language.

In the modern world, the practice of silence is both a challenge and a necessity. The constant influx of information, sound, and activity creates an energetic fragmentation, pulling the self away from its center. By consciously cultivating moments of silence, one reclaims the connection to the inner and outer flows of life, restoring balance and alignment.

Practical ways to integrate silence into daily life include:

Morning Stillness: Beginning the day with a few minutes of quiet, allowing the mind to settle and the body to align with the emanations of the new day.

Mindful Listening: Practicing active listening without interrupting or formulating a response, creating a space of silence within communication.

Technology Sabbaths: Setting aside regular periods without screens or devices, creating a sanctuary of quiet amidst the noise of modern life.

The wisdom of silence extends to creativity and decision-making. In moments of stillness, insights arise naturally, unburdened by the chatter of the mind. Many artists, writers, and thinkers have spoken of the inspiration that comes in silence, a flow of ideas that feels less like invention and more like discovery. This creative silence reflects the emanations of the universe, the infinite potential that lies within each quiet moment.

Silence is not an escape but a return—a homecoming to the essence of being. It is within silence that the truth of existence is revealed, not as a concept but as an experience. This truth is simple yet profound: that the self is not separate from the whole but an expression of it, a ripple in the vast ocean of life.

The practice of silence is a journey, one that deepens with time and intention. It begins with moments of quiet and expands into a way of being, a state of alignment with the flows of life. In silence, one finds not only peace but power—the ability to move with the currents of the universe, to act from a place of clarity and presence.

Through silence, one discovers the infinite within the finite, the stillness within the motion, the unity within the multiplicity. It is a reminder that the most profound truths are not spoken but felt, not seen but known. In embracing silence, one aligns with the emanations of life, becoming a vessel for the wisdom that flows through all things.

Silent wisdom is the essence of the cosmos, a presence that pervades every corner of existence. It is a guide, a teacher, a force of transformation and connection. To cultivate silence is to step into this wisdom, to become a living expression of the infinite quiet that sustains life.

Chapter 32
A Call to Unity

Beneath the surface of existence, where form and thought separate all things into distinct categories, a deeper truth hums. This truth is unity—the interconnectedness of all beings, energies, and emanations. The call to unity is not a distant cry but an ever-present resonance, echoing through the fabric of life. It is an invitation to remember, to align with the oneness that underpins every aspect of the cosmos.

Across cultures and traditions, the notion of unity has persisted, not as an abstract ideal but as an experienced reality. Indigenous wisdom speaks of the web of life, a network that ties each living thing to the other. Mystical traditions describe the dissolution of boundaries in states of enlightenment, where the self merges with the whole. Even modern science, through the study of quantum entanglement and morphic resonance, confirms the interconnectedness of particles and fields, offering evidence of this ancient understanding.

Unity begins with the awareness that all life shares the same source. Every emanation, every vibration, originates from the same primordial energy, expressing itself in countless forms. The diversity of existence, then, is not a contradiction to unity but a reflection of it, a demonstration of how the one becomes many while remaining whole.

The perception of separation is a necessary aspect of human experience, allowing the individual to navigate the physical world. Yet, it is also the root of division, conflict, and misunderstanding. To answer the call to unity is not to deny individuality but to transcend its limitations, to see beyond the apparent distinctions and recognize the shared essence that flows through all things.

The journey toward unity begins within. The human being is a microcosm of the universe, containing the same emanations that flow through the cosmos. To align with unity on a personal level is to harmonize these inner currents, bringing the body, mind, and spirit into a state of balance. This inner alignment creates a resonance that extends outward, connecting the individual to the greater web of life.

Practices for cultivating unity often emphasize presence and compassion. Mindfulness, the act of fully inhabiting each moment, dissolves the barriers between the observer and the observed, creating a sense of oneness with the flow of life. Acts of kindness and empathy expand this connection, bridging the gaps between self and other through the simple acknowledgment of shared humanity.

Unity is also experienced through the archetypes and symbols that appear across cultures. The Tree of Life, for instance, is a universal image that connects the heavens, earth, and underworld, illustrating the interdependence of all realms. The sacred circle, present in mandalas, medicine wheels, and other forms, represents wholeness and the cyclical nature of existence. These symbols serve as reminders of the unity that exists beneath the surface of diversity, guiding the seeker toward alignment with the greater whole.

In states of meditation or deep contemplation, the experience of unity becomes tangible. The boundaries of the self dissolve, and the individual becomes aware of their place within the infinite flow of emanations. This state is often described as one of profound peace and clarity, a direct encounter with the oneness that sustains all things.

Unity extends beyond the personal and spiritual realms into the collective. Communities, like individuals, are microcosms of the universe, their members interconnected by shared energies and intentions. When a group aligns with the call to unity, their collective energy amplifies, creating a field of resonance that extends far beyond their immediate surroundings. Practices such as group meditation, shared rituals, and collaborative creative endeavors foster this alignment, weaving individual threads into a unified tapestry.

On a planetary level, unity calls for a recognition of humanity's interdependence with the natural world. The earth is not merely a resource to be used but a living system of which all beings are a part. By attuning to the rhythms of the planet—the cycles of the seasons, the flows of water and air—one aligns with the emanations of the earth, becoming a steward of its well-being.

The challenges of the modern world often create a sense of disconnection, both from oneself and from others. Yet, these challenges also offer opportunities to rediscover unity. Acts of solidarity, whether in response to crisis or in pursuit of a shared vision, demonstrate the power of collective intention and remind humanity of its interconnectedness.

Practical ways to answer the call to unity include:

Shared Silence: Sitting in stillness with others, creating a field of resonance that connects each individual to the group and the greater whole.

Reciprocity with Nature: Engaging in acts of gratitude and care for the natural world, recognizing the mutual exchange of energy between humans and the earth.

Universal Prayer or Meditation: Focusing on the well-being of all beings, sending emanations of love and light into the world as a practice of unity.

Unity does not require the erasure of differences; rather, it celebrates them as expressions of the same source. Each culture, tradition, and perspective offers a unique lens through which the universal can be understood. To honor these differences is to honor the whole, to recognize that every part contributes to the harmony of the greater symphony.

The call to unity is not a distant goal but a present reality, accessible in every moment. It is heard in the stillness of meditation, in the connection between two people, in the beauty of a natural landscape. By attuning to this call, one aligns with the flows of life, becoming a living expression of the oneness that pervades the cosmos.

Through unity, the individual becomes whole, the community becomes harmonious, and the world becomes a reflection of the infinite. This is not a utopian vision but a profound truth, one that lies at the heart of existence. To answer the call is to step into this truth, to live as a vessel for the emanations of unity, and to contribute to the unfolding harmony of the universe.

The call to unity is eternal, a resonance that moves through every being, every moment, every breath. It is the thread that weaves the fabric of existence, the song that connects all voices. To embrace this call is to awaken to the deeper currents of life, to align with the sacred flow that sustains and transforms all things. In unity, there is no separation, only the infinite dance of the one and the many, the whole and its parts, the self and the cosmos.

Chapter 33
The Shared Journey

The path of life is rarely solitary, even when it appears so. Beneath the surface of individuality lies a profound interconnectedness that shapes every step, every choice, and every transformation. The shared journey of existence is not merely a metaphor but a reality, an intricate dance of energies and emanations that bind all beings to one another and to the greater whole.

Across the annals of time, humans have sought meaning not only in their individual lives but also in their collective existence. From the fires of ancient tribes to the temples of great civilizations, the recognition of shared purpose has been a cornerstone of human evolution. The act of gathering, whether for survival, worship, or celebration, reflects an innate understanding of the shared journey—a journey that transcends the self and merges with the greater flow of life.

The shared journey is both an internal and external phenomenon. Internally, it manifests as the recognition that one's thoughts, emotions, and actions are not isolated but ripple outward, affecting the larger energetic field. Externally, it is seen in the ways communities, families, and societies evolve together, their destinies intertwined. At its core, this journey is an expression of the universal truth of interconnectedness, a reminder that no one exists apart from the web of life.

The energetic nature of the shared journey is profound. Each individual carries a unique emanation, a frequency that contributes to the collective field. When these frequencies align, they create resonance, amplifying their power and coherence.

This resonance can be seen in moments of collective harmony, where groups achieve extraordinary feats, overcome immense challenges, or simply find peace in their shared presence.

In spiritual traditions, the shared journey is often depicted as a pilgrimage, a sacred undertaking that unites individuals in pursuit of a higher purpose. Whether walking the Camino de Santiago, circling the Kaaba, or participating in a vision quest, these acts embody the principle of shared intention. They remind participants that while the steps may be individual, the path is collective, and the destination is one of unity with the greater whole.

Rituals and ceremonies are powerful expressions of the shared journey. In these sacred acts, individuals come together to align their energies, creating a space where the boundaries between self and other dissolve. The chanting of mantras, the lighting of candles, the sharing of food—all these acts are more than symbolic. They are energetic practices that weave individual threads into a collective tapestry, strengthening the bonds that unite all participants.

The shared journey extends beyond human relationships to encompass all forms of life. The ecosystems of the natural world are a profound example of this principle. Each species, each element, plays a role in maintaining balance, its existence intertwined with countless others. The trees exchange oxygen for carbon dioxide with animals; the rivers sustain the land and its inhabitants; the sun nourishes all with its light. In this intricate web, no being is isolated, and the survival of the whole depends on the harmony of its parts.

In moments of crisis, the shared journey often becomes most visible. Disasters, both natural and human-made, reveal the profound interconnectedness of life. Acts of kindness, solidarity, and collective effort arise naturally in response, demonstrating the innate human capacity to align with the shared journey. These moments, though born of challenge, are opportunities for profound growth and healing, both for individuals and for the collective.

The shared journey is not without its challenges. The illusion of separation, fostered by ego and fear, often creates barriers to connection. Misunderstandings, conflicts, and divisions arise, threatening the harmony of the collective field. Yet, even these challenges are part of the journey, opportunities to learn, grow, and realign with the deeper truths of interconnectedness.

Practical ways to engage with the shared journey include:

Collaborative Practices: Participating in group meditations, shared rituals, or community service to align energies with others.

Active Listening: Fully hearing and understanding others without judgment, creating a space for genuine connection.

Conscious Contribution: Recognizing that every action, no matter how small, contributes to the collective field, and choosing to act with intention and awareness.

The shared journey is not confined to specific moments or events; it is a continuous flow that underlies all of existence. Every interaction, every relationship, every thought and action contributes to this journey, shaping the collective energy that moves through the world. To walk this path consciously is to recognize one's role in the greater whole, to align with the currents of life that flow through all things.

In the realm of energy and emanations, the shared journey is a powerful force for transformation. When individuals come together with aligned intentions, their combined energy transcends the sum of its parts, creating a field of possibility that can shape reality itself. This is seen in the phenomenon of collective intention, where groups focus their energies on healing, change, or creation, often achieving extraordinary results.

The shared journey also teaches humility and interdependence. It reminds each individual that their existence is not solitary but part of a vast network of relationships. This awareness fosters gratitude and compassion, qualities that strengthen the bonds of the shared journey and enhance the flow of emanations through the collective field.

At its highest expression, the shared journey is a reflection of the universal journey—the eternal dance of creation, destruction, and renewal that moves through all things. Each individual, each community, each species is a part of this cosmic journey, a thread in the infinite tapestry of existence. To walk this path consciously is to align with the deepest currents of life, to become a vessel for the emanations that sustain and transform the universe.

The shared journey is a call to remember, to awaken to the truth of interconnectedness and to act in harmony with it. It is an invitation to move beyond the self, to see and honor the divine in others, and to contribute to the unfolding evolution of the whole. In answering this call, one becomes a co-creator of the shared journey, a participant in the sacred dance of life that unites all beings, all energies, all emanations.

Chapter 34
The Flow of Forgiveness

Forgiveness is a current of profound transformation, an emanation that flows through the heart and spirit, cleansing and renewing all it touches. It is not merely an act or a gesture but a process, an energetic release that dissolves the dense vibrations of resentment, anger, and pain, allowing the soul to align with the higher flows of love and harmony.

Across cultures and traditions, forgiveness has been revered as a sacred practice, a gateway to freedom and transcendence. In the teachings of Buddhism, it is an essential element of compassion, the act of letting go of attachment to suffering. In Christianity, forgiveness is a path to divine grace, a way of embodying the love that transcends human limitation. In Indigenous traditions, it is a means of restoring balance, healing the wounds of conflict, and reconnecting with the web of life. These varied perspectives reveal forgiveness as a universal principle, an expression of the interconnectedness of all beings.

At its essence, forgiveness is an energetic process. When harm is inflicted, whether through words, actions, or circumstances, it leaves an imprint on the energetic field. This imprint, if unresolved, becomes a weight, a block that hinders the natural flow of life. Forgiveness acts as a transformative force, dissolving this weight and restoring the flow, both within the individual and between individuals.

The journey of forgiveness begins with awareness. To forgive, one must first acknowledge the presence of pain, anger, or resentment. These emotions, while often uncomfortable, are signals from the energetic body, indicating where healing is needed. By bringing awareness to these feelings, one begins the process of transformation, shifting from resistance to acceptance.

Forgiveness is often misunderstood as condoning or forgetting harm, but it is neither. It is not a denial of pain or injustice but an acknowledgment of it, followed by a conscious choice to release its hold. This release does not absolve the actions of others but liberates the self from the energetic bonds of the past, creating space for new possibilities.

The act of forgiveness is deeply personal, yet its effects ripple outward, touching the lives of others and the collective field. When one forgives, they contribute to the dissolution of negative energy patterns, breaking cycles of pain and retribution that perpetuate harm. This energetic shift creates a resonance of healing and reconciliation, opening pathways for greater harmony and understanding.

Forgiveness also extends to the self, a vital but often overlooked aspect of the process. The wounds of guilt, shame, and self-judgment can be as binding as those inflicted by others, creating dense emanations that block the flow of life. Self-forgiveness is an act of compassion, a recognition that one's mistakes are not the sum of their being but opportunities for growth and learning. By forgiving oneself, one restores the inner alignment that allows for greater connection with the world.

Rituals of forgiveness hold transformative power, serving as tangible expressions of the inner process. Writing a letter to someone who has caused pain, whether sent or unsent, allows the emotions to flow and be released. Lighting a candle or performing a symbolic act of letting go, such as burning the letter, amplifies the intention, channeling the emanations of forgiveness into the energetic field.

The heart is the center of forgiveness, the energetic gateway through which its transformative power flows. Practices that cultivate heart coherence, such as focused breathing, gratitude exercises, or meditative visualizations, strengthen the heart's field, creating a space for forgiveness to unfold. These practices align the heart with the higher frequencies of love and compassion, dissolving the lower vibrations of pain and resentment.

The flow of forgiveness also moves through time, reaching into the past to heal old wounds and extending into the future to prevent new ones. By forgiving ancestral traumas, whether personal or collective, one breaks the chains of inherited pain, freeing future generations from its weight. This work, though challenging, is an act of profound service, contributing to the evolution of the collective consciousness.

In relationships, forgiveness acts as a bridge, reconnecting hearts that have been divided by pain. It fosters understanding and empathy, dissolving the barriers of blame and judgment. Through forgiveness, relationships become spaces of healing and growth, where the shared journey is strengthened by the willingness to release and renew.

The flow of forgiveness also extends to the natural world. Humanity's relationship with the earth has been marked by harm and exploitation, leaving deep wounds in the planet's energetic field. Acts of reconciliation, such as ecological restoration, rituals of gratitude, or simply living with greater mindfulness, are forms of forgiveness that heal the bonds between humanity and the earth.

Practical techniques for cultivating forgiveness include:

Ho'oponopono: A traditional Hawaiian practice of reconciliation and healing, involving the repetition of phrases such as "I'm sorry, please forgive me, thank you, I love you."

Forgiveness Meditation: Visualizing the person, situation, or aspect of oneself to be forgiven, surrounding it with light and love, and releasing it into the flow of life.

Gratitude Practices: Shifting focus from pain to gratitude, acknowledging the lessons and growth that have arisen from challenging experiences.

The flow of forgiveness is not linear; it moves in waves, rising and falling as the process unfolds. There may be moments of resistance, where the pain feels too great to release, and moments of breakthrough, where the heart opens and the energy flows freely. This rhythm is natural, a reflection of the cyclical nature of healing and transformation.

Forgiveness is an act of liberation, not only for the one who forgives but for the world. Each act of forgiveness contributes to the dissolution of dense energies in the collective field, creating space for higher frequencies to emerge. It is a ripple that extends far beyond its point of origin, touching lives and hearts in unseen ways.

At its highest expression, forgiveness is an alignment with the universal emanations of love and compassion. It is a return to the flow of life, a recognition that pain and separation are but temporary disturbances in the infinite current of unity. Through forgiveness, one becomes a vessel for this flow, channeling its transformative power into the world.

The flow of forgiveness is a sacred journey, one that calls for courage, compassion, and trust. It is a reminder that healing is always possible, that the wounds of the past need not define the present or the future. By stepping into this flow, one aligns with the deeper truths of existence, becoming a living expression of the infinite capacity for renewal and transformation.

Chapter 35
Anchoring Light

Amidst the infinite emanations of existence, light stands as both the origin and the essence. It is the purest expression of energy, an eternal force that penetrates all dimensions of reality. To anchor light is to draw this primordial energy into the material plane, to align with its vibrations and allow it to illuminate, transform, and heal.

Throughout human history, light has been revered as a sacred element, a symbol of divine presence and cosmic truth. Ancient traditions across the globe have spoken of the importance of harnessing light, not only as a physical phenomenon but as a spiritual force. From the radiant halos of enlightened beings to the sacred fires of Vedic rituals, light is seen as the bridge between the earthly and the eternal, the visible and the unseen.

The process of anchoring light begins with recognition. Light is not external; it flows through every being, every form, every moment. It is the subtle essence that sustains life, the energy that animates the universe. To anchor it is to become aware of its presence, to consciously align with its currents and allow it to infuse every aspect of existence.

Light manifests in many forms, from the warmth of the sun to the luminous beauty of the stars, from the glow of a candle to the radiance of a loving heart. Each of these forms carries its own frequency, its own unique vibration, yet all are expressions of the same fundamental energy. By tuning into these frequencies, one begins to access the deeper flows of light, creating pathways for its anchoring.

The body itself is a vessel for light, a dynamic system of emanations that can channel and amplify its energy. Practices such as visualization, meditation, and breathwork are powerful tools for aligning the body with the flow of light. By visualizing the body as a luminous vessel, filled with and surrounded by radiant energy, one strengthens this connection, creating a field of light that extends into the world.

Sacred geometry, the patterns that underlie creation, serves as a gateway for anchoring light. Shapes such as the circle, the spiral, and the tetrahedron are not merely symbols but energetic structures that resonate with the vibrations of light. Meditating on these forms, creating them physically, or working with their energetic principles allows light to flow more freely, aligning the self with the harmony of the cosmos.

Rituals of light are ancient practices that bring this energy into focus. Lighting a candle, for instance, is more than an act of illumination; it is a ceremony, an invocation of the divine essence of light. Such rituals, whether simple or elaborate, create spaces where the emanations of light can be consciously anchored and directed.

The heart is the central channel for light within the human being. It is through the heart that the highest frequencies of love, compassion, and wisdom flow, emanating as light that touches and transforms. Practices that cultivate heart coherence, such as gratitude exercises and loving-kindness meditations, amplify this flow, turning the heart into a beacon of light that radiates into the world.

Anchoring light is not limited to personal practice; it is also a collective endeavor. When groups come together with shared intention, their combined energies create a powerful field that magnifies the flow of light. Group meditations, rituals, and acts of service are ways to anchor light on a larger scale, contributing to the healing and transformation of the collective field.

In the physical world, light interacts with matter to create color, a spectrum of vibrations that carry unique properties. Each color corresponds to specific frequencies of energy, influencing different aspects of being. Working with color consciously, whether through visualization, art, or environment design, allows for a deeper connection to the emanations of light, enhancing their transformative power.

The anchoring of light is also a deeply creative process. Artists, musicians, and writers often speak of being "illuminated" by inspiration, a flow of ideas and energy that seems to come from beyond. This illumination is the light of creation, a force that moves through the individual and manifests as beauty, truth, and meaning. To anchor light is to become a co-creator with the universe, channeling its energy into forms that uplift and inspire.

Light has the power to heal, to dissolve dense energies and restore harmony. In practices such as Reiki and other energy healing modalities, practitioners work directly with the emanations of light, channeling them into the body to remove blockages and activate the natural flow of life force. Visualizing light entering the body, filling areas of pain or tension, and radiating outward is a simple yet profound method of self-healing.

The natural world is a profound source of light, both physical and energetic. The sun, as the primary source of life on Earth, is a direct channel of cosmic light. Practices such as sun gazing (when done safely), spending time in natural sunlight, or simply connecting with the rhythms of day and night align the self with this fundamental energy.

Crystals and minerals, formed over millennia within the Earth, are physical anchors of light. Their structures allow them to hold and transmit specific frequencies, making them powerful tools for working with light. Placing crystals in meditation spaces, carrying them, or using them in energy work enhances the flow of light, amplifying its presence and effects.

In moments of darkness, both literal and metaphorical, the practice of anchoring light becomes even more essential. Light is not the absence of darkness but its transformation, a force that reveals, clarifies, and heals. By consciously anchoring light in challenging times, one creates a pathway for hope and renewal, both for oneself and others.

Anchoring light is an act of service to the world. Each individual who aligns with this practice becomes a source of illumination, contributing to the collective field and inspiring others to do the same. This service extends beyond human connections, touching the Earth itself, the plants, animals, and all forms of life that share its space.

To anchor light is to live as a bridge between dimensions, a conduit for the sacred energy that flows through all things. It is a practice of alignment, a way of being that turns the ordinary into the extraordinary, the seen into the unseen. Through this practice, one becomes a living expression of the light, a beacon of its transformative power.

The light that is anchored does not belong to any individual; it is universal, infinite, and eternal. Each act of anchoring contributes to the unfolding of the greater harmony, the divine order that moves through all existence. To anchor light is to participate in this unfolding, to become a co-creator of the luminous tapestry of life.

In the anchoring of light, the boundaries between self and cosmos dissolve. The individual becomes the infinite, the finite becomes the eternal, and the dance of creation continues, illuminated by the light that sustains it all.

Chapter 36
Lunar Reconnection

The moon, ever-present in the sky, holds a timeless resonance within the human spirit. Its cycles are mirrors of life's rhythms, a celestial rhythm that governs tides, seasons, and the flow of energies within all living beings. To reconnect with the moon is to align oneself with these natural cycles, to step into a profound relationship with the ebb and flow of life's emanations.

Ancient civilizations revered the moon as a luminous guardian of the night, attributing to it the qualities of mystery, intuition, and transformation. Temples dedicated to lunar deities such as Selene, Chandra, and Khonsu bore witness to humanity's deep connection with its phases. Even in contemporary times, the moon's cycles remain woven into cultural practices, from agricultural calendars to spiritual observances. These traditions reflect an enduring truth: the moon is not merely a celestial body but a force of influence and guidance.

The phases of the moon—new, waxing, full, and waning—each carry distinct energetic emanations. These phases are not abstract concepts but dynamic flows of energy that interact with the Earth and its inhabitants. By attuning to these phases, one aligns with the natural rhythm of creation and dissolution, harnessing the moon's power to enhance intention, reflection, and transformation.

The new moon, dark and hidden from view, represents beginnings and potential. Its energy is one of stillness and renewal, a time to plant seeds both literal and metaphorical. During this phase, the emanations of the moon are subtle yet potent, inviting introspection and the setting of intentions. It is a time to look inward, to identify desires and goals, and to align with the cycles of growth that will follow.

As the moon waxes, its energy builds, growing stronger and more vibrant with each passing night. This phase is a period of action and manifestation, where intentions set during the new moon begin to take shape. The waxing moon's emanations support creativity, effort, and expansion, encouraging movement toward one's goals.

The full moon, radiant and whole, is the culmination of the lunar cycle, a time of heightened energy and illumination. Under its light, emotions, thoughts, and intentions come to the surface, often with great clarity. The full moon's emanations amplify all that they touch, making this phase ideal for reflection, celebration, and the release of what no longer serves. It is a time to honor achievements, express gratitude, and let go of any burdens that hinder growth.

As the moon wanes, its light diminishes, and its energy turns inward once more. This phase is one of release and preparation, a time to shed the old and make space for the new. The waning moon supports practices of cleansing, forgiveness, and rest, allowing for integration and renewal.

The moon's cycles are deeply connected to the human experience, particularly the rhythms of the body and emotions. The lunar influence on water is well-documented, from the tides of the ocean to the subtle movements of water within living organisms. Given that the human body is largely composed of water, the moon's emanations have a profound impact on physical and emotional states. Recognizing and working with these rhythms allows for greater harmony and balance.

Rituals and practices for lunar reconnection are as diverse as the cultures that honor the moon. These practices often involve elements that resonate with the moon's qualities: water, silver, reflective surfaces, and symbols of cycles and change. Simple acts such as moon gazing, journaling by moonlight, or creating altars with lunar symbols foster a deeper connection with the moon's energy.

Meditative practices aligned with the moon's phases deepen this connection. During the new moon, visualization exercises focused on planting seeds of intention align the practitioner with the energy of beginnings. The waxing moon invites movement-based meditations, such as dance or yoga, to harness its dynamic energy. The full moon's energy is ideal for contemplative meditation, focusing on clarity and release. The waning moon supports grounding practices, such as breathwork or gentle walks in nature, to align with its inward flow.

The moon's cycles are not limited to individual experience but extend to the collective. Festivals such as the Mid-Autumn Festival, the Hindu celebration of Karva Chauth, and the Islamic observance of Ramadan's crescent moons illustrate the moon's role in uniting communities. These gatherings serve as powerful expressions of lunar reconnection, amplifying the moon's emanations through shared intention and celebration.

The moon also reflects the interplay of light and shadow, a dynamic that mirrors the human journey. Its phases remind us that growth and transformation require both illumination and darkness. The hidden face of the new moon is as vital as the glowing orb of the full moon, just as moments of introspection and release are essential to personal evolution.

Astrologically, the moon is associated with intuition, emotions, and the subconscious mind. Its position in a natal chart reveals insights into one's emotional nature and inner world. Working with these astrological insights enhances lunar reconnection, providing a framework for understanding how the moon's cycles interact with individual energies.

In reconnecting with the moon, one also reconnects with the Earth and its rhythms. The lunar cycle governs the tides, influences plant growth, and synchronizes with the reproductive cycles of many species. By aligning with these natural rhythms, one fosters a deeper sense of belonging and stewardship for the planet.

The moon's influence extends beyond the physical to the spiritual and energetic realms. In esoteric traditions, the moon is seen as a portal, a bridge between the material and the ethereal. Its emanations are said to enhance psychic abilities, dreams, and spiritual insight, making it a powerful ally for those seeking to explore the unseen dimensions of existence.

Practical steps for lunar reconnection include:

Moon Journaling: Tracking thoughts, emotions, and experiences throughout the lunar cycle to observe patterns and align with its phases.

Lunar Water Rituals: Placing water under the moonlight to absorb its emanations, then using this water for cleansing or intention-setting practices.

Night Walks: Spending time outdoors under the moon, allowing its light and energy to flow through the body and spirit.

The moon's cycles are a reminder of life's constant motion, its patterns of growth, culmination, and renewal. Reconnecting with these cycles is not merely a return to ancient practices but a reawakening to the wisdom of nature and the cosmos. Through this reconnection, one becomes attuned to the flows of life, aligned with the rhythms that sustain and transform.

Lunar reconnection is a dance with the infinite, a reminder that light and shadow are partners in creation. By stepping into this dance, one aligns with the sacred flows of existence, becoming a vessel for the moon's emanations and a participant in the eternal cycles of life.

Chapter 37
Energetic Shields

The unseen forces that move through the universe are both nourishing and challenging. Among the flows of life are currents of discord, emanations of disharmony that, if left unchecked, can disrupt the balance of the self. Energetic shields are a sacred practice, an ancient art designed to protect and preserve the integrity of one's energetic field while maintaining openness to the harmonious emanations of the universe.

Every living being has an inherent energetic boundary, a subtle field that surrounds and defines its essence. This boundary, often called the aura, acts as a buffer between the individual and the surrounding energies. It filters what enters and exits, maintaining equilibrium within. However, this natural shield can be compromised by emotional stress, physical exhaustion, environmental factors, or the dense emanations of others. To consciously create and maintain energetic shields is to safeguard this boundary, ensuring resilience and balance in the face of life's challenges.

The need for energetic shielding has been recognized across cultures and traditions. Indigenous shamans envelop themselves in protective rituals before engaging with the spirit world. Buddhist monks visualize luminous spheres of light as barriers against negativity. In Western esotericism, the practice of "casting a circle" creates a sacred space impenetrable to harmful energies. Though their forms vary, these practices share a common purpose: to fortify the energetic field and align it with the higher frequencies of protection and harmony.

Energetic shields are not walls; they are dynamic emanations, living extensions of the self. They adapt to the flow of energy, allowing what is beneficial to enter while deflecting or transforming that which is harmful. This adaptability is essential, for a rigid barrier can isolate and constrict, whereas a fluid shield maintains connection and openness.

The creation of an energetic shield begins with intention. The act of declaring one's desire for protection sets the foundation for the shield, aligning the self with the frequencies of safety and resilience. Intention acts as the seed from which the shield grows, its emanations strengthened by focus and clarity.

Visualization is a powerful tool in constructing energetic shields. By imagining a radiant sphere of light surrounding the body, one creates a tangible energetic boundary. The color and texture of the shield can be adapted to suit specific needs: gold for strength, white for purity, blue for calm, or a reflective surface to deflect negativity. Each visualization carries its own vibration, shaping the shield's qualities and functions.

Breath is another essential element in the creation of energetic shields. The rhythmic flow of inhalation and exhalation generates waves of energy that amplify the shield's presence. By synchronizing visualization with breath, one infuses the shield with vitality, reinforcing its emanations with each cycle of life force.

Crystals and sacred objects serve as anchors for energetic shields. Stones such as black tourmaline, obsidian, and amethyst are renowned for their protective properties, their structures resonating with frequencies that deflect or neutralize harmful energies. Carrying or wearing these stones, placing them in one's environment, or using them in meditation strengthens the energetic field, enhancing its natural defenses.

Sacred rituals further empower energetic shields, creating a focused space for their formation and maintenance. Lighting incense or sage, reciting mantras or affirmations, and engaging in ceremonial acts such as anointing with oil or water imbue the shield with sacred intent. These rituals not only protect but also sanctify, aligning the individual with the higher emanations of divine protection.

Energetic shielding extends beyond the self, encompassing spaces and environments. Homes, workplaces, and communal areas can be energetically fortified, creating sanctuaries that repel discord and foster harmony. Techniques such as cleansing with sound or smoke, placing protective symbols or objects, and setting boundaries with intentional words or actions establish energetic shields for spaces, ensuring that they remain balanced and uplifting.

One of the most profound forms of shielding arises from the heart. The heart's electromagnetic field is the strongest in the body, radiating far beyond physical boundaries. By cultivating love, gratitude, and compassion, one amplifies this field, creating a natural shield that repels dense energies and attracts harmonious emanations. This heart-centered shield is not merely defensive; it is transformative, transmuting negativity into light.

In the modern world, the need for energetic shielding has grown. The constant influx of information, the pressures of urban environments, and the pervasive presence of electromagnetic fields can overwhelm the natural boundaries of the self. Conscious shielding practices provide a sanctuary amidst this chaos, offering a means to reclaim balance and serenity.

Practical techniques for energetic shielding include:

The Mirror Shield: Visualizing a reflective surface around the body that deflects negative energy while allowing positive energy to flow freely.

The Golden Egg: Imagining oneself encased in an egg of radiant gold light, a shield of strength and protection.

Mantric Shielding: Repeating protective affirmations or mantras, such as "I am safe, I am protected, I am surrounded by light," to reinforce the energetic boundary.

Energetic shields are not static; they require care and renewal. Just as the body benefits from rest and nourishment, so too does the energetic field. Regular practices of grounding, cleansing, and meditation sustain the shield's vitality, ensuring its effectiveness over time.

The interplay between shielding and openness is a delicate balance. While protection is essential, it must not lead to isolation. An over-reliance on shielding can create barriers that inhibit connection and growth. The true art of shielding lies in its fluidity, its ability to safeguard without separating, to protect without constraining.

At its highest expression, energetic shielding is not an act of defense but one of alignment. It is a declaration of one's sovereignty, a commitment to preserving the integrity of one's being while remaining connected to the greater whole. Through this practice, one becomes both grounded and expansive, anchored in their essence yet open to the infinite flows of life.

Energetic shields are a reflection of the self, a manifestation of one's intention, focus, and resonance. They are tools of empowerment, reminders of the boundless potential within to shape and direct the currents of energy. In creating and maintaining these shields, one steps into the role of co-creator, an active participant in the dance of emanations that sustains existence.

Through the practice of energetic shielding, one cultivates resilience, harmony, and connection. It is a practice that honors the self, the sacred space within, and the greater web of life. To shield is to embrace the dual truth of existence: the need for protection and the infinite capacity for connection, united in the flow of energy that binds all things.

Chapter 38
Transcendental Journey

The transcendental journey is the path of venturing beyond the physical senses into realms where the unseen and the infinite converge. It is a voyage into the depths of consciousness, where the boundaries of the material world dissolve, revealing dimensions of pure emanation and profound connection. This journey, taken by mystics, seekers, and shamans across time, is not an escape from reality but an expansion into its most fundamental truths.

Humanity's fascination with altered states of consciousness spans cultures and epochs. From the ecstatic trances of the ancient Greek oracles to the meditative stillness of Zen practitioners, these transcendental states have been pursued as gateways to divine wisdom, healing, and self-discovery. They are the bridges between the ordinary and the extraordinary, the tangible and the transcendent.

To embark on a transcendental journey is to shift from the external to the internal, to access the subtle currents of energy that flow through the self and the cosmos. This shift is not a departure but a deepening, a realignment with the emanations that connect all existence. The tools for this journey—breath, sound, intention—are simple yet profound, opening pathways to realms that exist beyond the reach of the ordinary mind.

Breath is the foundation of transcendence. The rhythm of inhalation and exhalation is a microcosm of the universal flow, the endless cycle of expansion and contraction. Practices such as pranayama, rebirthing breathwork, or holotropic breathing activate this flow, altering states of consciousness and awakening the energy centers within. Through breath, the body becomes a vessel for transcendence, a conduit for the infinite.

Sound is another gateway to transcendental states, its vibrations resonating with the subtle frequencies of the cosmos. Chanting mantras, listening to binaural beats, or engaging with harmonic instruments such as singing bowls or gongs align the mind and body with these frequencies, dissolving barriers and opening portals to higher dimensions. Sound is not merely heard; it is felt, its emanations penetrating deeply into the being.

Meditation is the cornerstone of transcendental practice, a method of stilling the surface mind to access the depths of awareness. Techniques such as focused attention, mindfulness, or visualization guide the practitioner inward, where the layers of thought and identity peel away, revealing the essence of pure being. In this state, time and space lose their grip, replaced by a sense of infinite presence.

The transcendental journey is not confined to stillness; movement can also be a path to altered states. Practices such as ecstatic dance, Tai Chi, or shamanic drumming engage the body in a dynamic flow, creating a rhythm that mirrors the cycles of the universe. Through movement, the physical and energetic bodies align, opening pathways to transcendental experiences.

Rituals and ceremonies hold a sacred space for transcendence, their symbols and actions designed to bridge the material and the spiritual. Whether through the use of sacred plants, guided journeys, or communal practices, these ceremonies create environments where the veil between worlds thins, allowing for direct encounters with the unseen.

The transcendental journey is deeply personal, yet it also connects to the collective. Mystical traditions speak of the Akashic records, the universal field of knowledge and memory accessible through altered states. In such states, individuals often report encounters with archetypal beings, shared symbols, or collective truths, suggesting that the transcendental experience is not isolated but part of a larger web of consciousness.

The practice of astral travel or out-of-body experiences exemplifies the transcendental journey's expansive nature. Through focused intention and relaxation, practitioners describe leaving their physical bodies to explore realms of pure energy and light. These experiences, though deeply individual, often share common elements, such as encounters with luminous beings, vivid landscapes, and a profound sense of interconnectedness.

Dreams are another dimension of transcendental exploration, their symbolic language offering insights into the unconscious and beyond. Lucid dreaming, the practice of becoming aware within a dream, allows for conscious navigation of these realms. In dreams, the boundaries of reality blur, revealing truths that elude the waking mind.

The transcendental journey is not without challenges. The unknown can be both awe-inspiring and intimidating, its vastness requiring courage and trust. Encounters with shadow aspects of the self, intense emotions, or unfamiliar energies may arise, testing the practitioner's resolve. These challenges are not obstacles but opportunities for growth, invitations to integrate and transform.

Integration is an essential part of the transcendental journey. The insights and experiences gained in altered states must be brought back into the material world, where they can manifest as wisdom, healing, or creative expression. Practices such as journaling, art, or sharing with others help ground these experiences, ensuring that they contribute to the journey of the soul.

Modern science has begun to explore the transcendental journey, its tools and methods shedding light on ancient practices. Research on brainwave states, neuroplasticity, and the effects of meditation and breathwork reveal the physiological basis of altered states. Psychedelic studies, once shunned, are uncovering their potential for healing trauma, expanding consciousness, and fostering spiritual connection.

The transcendental journey is ultimately a return to the self, a recognition that the vastness of the cosmos resides within.

It dissolves the illusion of separation, revealing a reality where all is interconnected, where the self is both a drop and the ocean. In this state, the individual becomes a vessel for the emanations of the infinite, channeling its energy into the world.

Practical techniques for embarking on a transcendental journey include:

Guided Visualization: Using imagery to journey inward, such as envisioning a path through a forest or ascending a staircase into light.

Shamanic Drumming: Listening to repetitive drumbeats to induce a trance state, facilitating travel to non-ordinary realms.

Floatation Therapy: Immersing oneself in sensory isolation tanks to access deep meditative states.

The transcendental journey is not a destination but a practice, a continuous unfolding of awareness. It is a path that invites exploration and discovery, where each step reveals new dimensions of existence. Through this journey, one aligns with the flow of the infinite, becoming both witness and participant in the sacred dance of creation.

To journey transcendentally is to embrace the unknown, to trust in the currents of life that carry the soul beyond the familiar. It is an act of courage, a declaration of the spirit's desire to expand and evolve. In this journey, the self is both the traveler and the destination, the finite and the infinite united in the boundless emanations of being.

Chapter 39
Voices of the Cosmos

The cosmos speaks in languages both subtle and profound, resonating across dimensions and permeating the boundaries of perception. These voices are not mere metaphors but genuine emanations—energetic transmissions that flow through the fabric of existence, carrying messages, guidance, and insights. To attune to these voices is to open a dialogue with the infinite, to bridge the seen and unseen realms in a communion that transcends the ordinary.

Throughout human history, individuals and cultures have sought to interpret the voices of the cosmos. Ancient civilizations, such as the Babylonians, Egyptians, and Mayans, observed celestial movements and translated them into intricate systems of meaning. Shamans listened to the whispers of the wind and the rhythms of the earth, perceiving messages that informed their communities. Prophets, mystics, and seers claimed to hear divine guidance, their words shaping the spiritual narratives of entire civilizations.

Channeling is one of the most direct ways of engaging with these voices. It is the practice of allowing one's consciousness to align with higher intelligences, serving as a vessel through which their messages flow. Channelers report connections with spiritual guides, ancestors, or universal consciousness itself, often describing these experiences as deeply transformative. The messages received are not confined to words; they may manifest as images, sensations, or streams of pure knowing.

The process of channeling begins with intention and openness. It requires the practitioner to quiet the mind, attune to subtle frequencies, and create a space where communication can occur. Techniques such as meditation, breathwork, and focused visualization help align the practitioner's energetic field with the vibratory patterns of the cosmos, facilitating this connection.

Mediumship, a form of channeling, focuses specifically on communication with spirits of the departed. Mediums act as bridges between the physical and spiritual realms, relaying messages from those who have passed on. While often misunderstood or dismissed, this practice has been integral to many cultures, providing comfort, closure, and insights to those seeking connection with their ancestors or loved ones.

In addition to personal practices, sacred texts across cultures have been considered conduits of cosmic voices. From the Vedas to the Quran, from the Tao Te Ching to the Bible, these writings are revered as channels of divine wisdom. Their creation is often attributed to moments of profound inspiration or revelation, where the boundaries between the individual and the infinite dissolve.

The voices of the cosmos also manifest through natural phenomena. The rustling of leaves, the hum of bees, the crash of ocean waves—these are not random sounds but expressions of the universal symphony. Indigenous traditions often emphasize listening to nature as a way to receive guidance, interpreting its rhythms and patterns as messages from the Earth and beyond.

Dreams are another realm where cosmic voices emerge. In the dream state, the conscious mind loosens its grip, allowing messages from the subconscious and the universal field to surface. Dreams can be symbolic, offering insights through archetypal imagery, or direct, delivering clear guidance or warnings. Lucid dreaming enhances this process, enabling conscious interaction with the messages of the dream world.

The practice of automatic writing is a powerful method for engaging with cosmic voices. In this state, the practitioner allows words to flow onto the page without conscious direction, often entering a trance-like state where messages emerge unfiltered. These writings are sometimes poetic, prophetic, or deeply personal, reflecting the wisdom of the source they channel.

Cosmic voices are not limited to guidance; they are also expressions of creative inspiration. Artists, musicians, and writers often describe their work as being "channeled," a flow of ideas and visions that seem to originate beyond the self. This creative force, whether called the muse, universal mind, or divine inspiration, is a profound expression of the cosmos speaking through human vessels.

Science, too, can be seen as a dialogue with the cosmos. The discovery of universal laws, the exploration of quantum phenomena, and the search for extraterrestrial intelligence are all ways of interpreting the cosmic language. The structure of DNA, the geometry of galaxies, and the resonance of particles reveal a universe imbued with intelligence and order, its voices encoded in the very fabric of reality.

Ethical discernment is vital when engaging with cosmic voices. Not all messages resonate with truth or alignment. The practitioner must cultivate clarity, grounding, and an unwavering connection to their inner knowing to differentiate between authentic guidance and distortions. Practices such as grounding meditation, protective visualizations, and alignment with higher intentions safeguard the integrity of these connections.

The act of listening to the cosmos is inherently transformative. It requires the practitioner to expand their awareness, to step beyond the confines of the ordinary and into the vastness of existence. This expansion often brings profound shifts in perception, dissolving illusions of separation and revealing the interconnectedness of all things.

Practical techniques for engaging with the voices of the cosmos include:

Tuning to Nature: Spending time in natural environments, listening deeply to the sounds, patterns, and emanations of the Earth.

Meditative Inquiry: Entering meditation with a specific question or intention, allowing insights or messages to arise organically.

Symbolic Interpretation: Keeping a journal of synchronicities, dreams, or recurring symbols, reflecting on their deeper meanings.

The voices of the cosmos are not confined to the extraordinary; they are woven into the fabric of everyday life. A chance encounter, a fragment of a song, or an intuitive nudge can carry profound meaning, guiding the individual along their path. The key lies in cultivating awareness, in recognizing these moments as part of the cosmic dialogue.

To listen to the voices of the cosmos is to remember one's place within the vast tapestry of existence. It is an act of humility and empowerment, a recognition that the universe speaks not only to us but through us. In opening to these voices, one becomes both the listener and the message, a living expression of the infinite emanations that sustain and transform all things.

Chapter 40
Seeds of Intention

Every action, thought, and emotion begins as a seed of intention, an invisible emanation born from the depths of consciousness. These seeds carry immense creative potential, shaping reality as they unfold. Intention is not merely desire or wish—it is the focused alignment of energy with purpose, the spark that initiates transformation in the seen and unseen realms.

Ancient traditions understood the power of intention as a force of creation. In Hinduism, the Sanskrit term **Sankalpa** refers to a solemn vow or intention, a mental resolve rooted in alignment with higher truth. Indigenous practices often involve ceremonial acts to imbue intentions with the sacred, using chants, symbols, or offerings to activate their power. These practices reveal a timeless understanding: intention is the bridge between thought and manifestation, a tool for harmonizing the inner and outer worlds.

The potency of intention lies in its resonance. It emanates from the heart, the mind, and the energetic body, sending ripples through the universal field. Like a stone cast into a still lake, a clear and focused intention generates waves that influence and interact with the currents of existence. These waves are not bound by time or space; they traverse dimensions, connecting the self with the infinite.

For an intention to take root and flourish, it must be nurtured with clarity. Vagueness dilutes its potency, while precision strengthens its resonance. The act of clearly defining one's intention—whether through words, visualization, or symbolic representation—acts as a signal to the cosmos, declaring one's alignment with a specific frequency of creation.

The process of planting a seed of intention begins with stillness. In moments of quiet reflection, the noise of external distractions fades, allowing the subtle whisper of the soul to emerge. This whisper is the essence of true intention, free from egoic desires or fleeting impulses. It is the voice of the deeper self, attuned to the flows of life and aligned with higher purpose.

Visualization amplifies the power of intention. By vividly imagining the desired outcome as if it has already manifested, one infuses the intention with emotion and energy. This act of envisioning creates a blueprint in the energetic field, a template for the physical manifestation to follow. The more detailed and sensory-rich the visualization, the stronger its resonance with the universal flow.

Emotion acts as the lifeblood of intention. The feelings of joy, gratitude, or love associated with the desired outcome elevate its frequency, aligning it with the harmonious currents of creation. Negative or resistant emotions, on the other hand, act as barriers, inhibiting the flow of energy. By cultivating emotional alignment with the intention, one ensures that its emanations remain strong and unimpeded.

Sacred rituals serve as vessels for intentions, transforming them into tangible acts of creation. Lighting a candle, planting a tree, or crafting an object imbued with symbolic meaning anchors the intention in the material realm, creating a focal point for its energy. These rituals not only honor the intention but also serve as reminders of one's commitment to its manifestation.

The alignment of intention with natural cycles enhances its potency. The phases of the moon, the changing seasons, and the rhythms of the sun and stars are all expressions of universal flow. By attuning intentions to these cycles—planting seeds during the new moon, releasing old patterns during the waning moon, or setting goals at the solstice—one aligns with the larger forces of creation, amplifying the intention's power.

The practice of written intention, such as journaling or crafting affirmations, channels thoughts into structured form, grounding their energy. Writing an intention crystallizes its essence, transforming it from a fleeting thought into a physical artifact. Affirmations, repeated with conviction, reinforce the intention, embedding it deeply into the subconscious mind and the energetic field.

Intention is not limited to the individual; it is a collective force capable of shaping communities and the world. Group meditations, prayer circles, and collaborative rituals harness the power of shared intention, magnifying its emanations. When multiple hearts and minds align with a common purpose, their combined energy creates a resonance that transcends individual limitations, influencing the collective consciousness.

Scientific studies on the power of intention, such as those conducted in the fields of quantum physics and consciousness research, reveal intriguing insights. Experiments on the observer effect suggest that focused attention can influence outcomes at the quantum level. Studies on collective intention, such as the Global Consciousness Project, hint at the interconnected nature of thought and reality, demonstrating measurable shifts in global energy during synchronized meditative efforts.

The challenges of intention lie not in its creation but in its nurturing. Doubt, fear, and impatience can act as weeds, stifling the growth of the seed before it has a chance to flourish. Trust is the soil in which intentions grow—trust in oneself, in the process, and in the universal flow. By releasing attachment to the outcome and surrendering to the unfolding journey, one allows the intention to manifest in its highest and most aligned form.

To cultivate the art of intention is to cultivate the art of creation. It is a practice of mindful awareness, of recognizing the power within to shape and direct the currents of life. It requires courage to dream, discipline to focus, and faith to trust in the unseen forces that guide the process.

Practical techniques for working with seeds of intention include:

Daily Intentions: Beginning each day with a clear intention, focusing on qualities or outcomes to embody throughout the day.

Vision Boards: Creating a visual representation of intentions using images, symbols, and words that resonate with the desired outcomes.

Gratitude Practices: Expressing gratitude as if the intention has already manifested, aligning emotions with the frequency of fulfillment.

The power of intention lies not only in its ability to create but in its ability to transform. It is a tool for aligning with one's highest self, for cultivating clarity, and for fostering connection with the greater whole. Through intention, one becomes an active participant in the dance of existence, a co-creator in the unfolding story of the cosmos.

The seeds of intention are sacred, their emanations echoing through the dimensions of time and space. In planting them, one honors the creative force within and the boundless potential of the universe. To nurture these seeds is to nurture the self, the Earth, and the infinite web of life, ensuring that the fruits of intention blossom into their fullest and most luminous forms.

Chapter 41
The Web of Life

The interconnected web of existence reveals itself not only as a philosophical concept but as a palpable truth that underpins all life. This intricate tapestry is woven from threads of energy, linking every being, every element, and every thought in a vast, unseen network. It is not a mere metaphor but a living reality, vibrating with the resonance of countless emanations that pulse through the cosmos.

This web is ancient, predating human understanding, yet it permeates our awareness in subtle ways. It is present in the murmuration of birds, the synchronized movement of schools of fish, and the unspoken connection shared between humans and the natural world. Indigenous traditions across the globe have long recognized this interconnectedness. They speak of the Earth as a living entity, its breath the wind, its veins the rivers, its heart the molten core from which life draws sustenance.

In modern times, scientific exploration has unveiled evidence of this energetic web. Studies on plant communication, for example, reveal how trees and fungi share resources and information through underground networks, a phenomenon described as the "Wood Wide Web." Quantum physics introduces us to entanglement, the uncanny connection between particles separated by vast distances, behaving as though they are one. These discoveries align seamlessly with ancient understandings, bridging the gap between mysticism and empirical observation.

The energetic web is not confined to the material plane. It extends into the subtle realms, encompassing emotions, thoughts, and intentions. When one individual experiences joy, sorrow, or fear, these emanations ripple outward, influencing the energetic field of others. Collective consciousness arises from this interplay, a shared frequency born of innumerable vibrations. It explains how societal movements gain momentum and why certain places hold profound energetic imprints of historical events.

Attuning oneself to the web of life begins with awareness. The first step is to cultivate sensitivity to the subtle connections that bind us to the world around us. This practice often starts in nature, where the web is most visible. The rustling of leaves in the wind, the rhythmic crashing of waves, and the quiet hum of a forest at dusk—all are manifestations of the web's pulsations. By immersing oneself in these environments, one begins to sense the subtle flows of energy that sustain and connect all living things.

Breathing exercises provide a powerful means of aligning with this web. By synchronizing one's breath with natural rhythms—such as the rising and falling of tides or the phases of the moon—one attunes to the greater cycles of life. Conscious breathing not only enhances physical vitality but also deepens the sense of unity with the larger whole.

Meditative practices further sharpen the perception of the web. Sitting in stillness, focusing on the energetic currents within and around the body, one can begin to feel the subtle threads of connection. Visualizing these threads as luminous strands linking oneself to all beings fosters a profound sense of interconnectedness. This practice dissolves the illusion of separation, revealing the self as a node within the infinite web.

The web of life is not a static structure; it is dynamic, constantly shifting and evolving. Just as a spider adjusts its web to respond to changes in its environment, so too does the energetic web adapt to the flow of life. When harm is inflicted upon one part of the web—be it environmental destruction, societal unrest, or personal discord—the entire network feels the strain. Conversely, acts of healing and harmony resonate outward, strengthening the web and restoring balance.

Working consciously with the web involves both receiving and giving. To receive is to open oneself to the guidance, support, and wisdom that flow through the web. This may manifest as intuitive insights, synchronicities, or a deep sense of knowing. To give is to contribute positive energy to the web through thoughts, words, and actions. Even small gestures, such as planting a tree, offering a kind word, or engaging in mindful prayer, send ripples of healing through the network.

The role of community in the web cannot be overstated. Human connections are among the most potent threads within this tapestry. When individuals come together with a shared intention—whether in ceremony, celebration, or collective action—their combined energy amplifies, creating a powerful resonance that transcends the individual. This collective vibration has the potential to heal wounds, inspire transformation, and elevate consciousness.

One must also recognize the web's capacity to reflect. Just as a drop of dew on a spider's web mirrors the light of the sun, so too does the web reflect the energies we project into it. This reflection is not punitive but instructive, offering opportunities for growth and realignment. If one encounters discord or disharmony in the web, it serves as an invitation to examine and adjust one's inner state.

Practical exercises for engaging with the web include:

Energetic Mapping: Visualize the web of connections extending from your body to all living beings, places, and elements. Observe how energy flows through this network and identify areas where it feels strong or weak.

Reciprocal Giving: Offer gratitude to the web through acts of kindness, rituals, or meditation, and remain open to receiving its blessings in return.

Harmonic Tuning: Use sound, such as singing bowls, chants, or natural tones, to harmonize with the web's frequencies.

Modern technology, though often perceived as a barrier to the web, can also serve as a bridge. Online communities, when aligned with purpose and integrity, can create virtual threads that mirror the physical and energetic connections of the web. The challenge lies in using these tools consciously, ensuring that they enhance rather than disrupt the natural flow of energy.

The web of life invites us to remember our place within the greater whole. It calls us to move beyond the illusion of separation and embrace the reality of interdependence. By nurturing the web, we nurture ourselves, for we are not separate from it—we are it. Through mindful participation, we become co-creators of a world where harmony, balance, and unity prevail.

To honor the web is to honor the essence of life itself. It is a sacred dance of connection, a symphony of emanations weaving through time and space. By embracing this truth, we awaken to the infinite beauty and potential of the web and our integral role within its design.

Chapter 42
Residual Energy

Within every space and object lies a silent witness to history. Residual energy, the imprint left by moments both monumental and mundane, saturates the environments we inhabit and the objects we hold dear. These energetic echoes persist, often unnoticed, yet their influence shapes our perceptions, emotions, and even physical well-being. The study and conscious interaction with residual energy open a doorway to understanding the energetic layers of our reality.

Ancient traditions have long acknowledged the presence of such energies. Temples, burial sites, and ceremonial spaces were deliberately chosen and prepared to amplify positive vibrations and preserve sacred intentions. Conversely, places of suffering—battlefields, prisons, and homes marked by discord—carry denser imprints, often described as haunting or oppressive. These energies are not bound to specific forms but exist as unseen traces that interact with the living.

Science provides glimpses into this phenomenon. Research into water memory and crystalline structures suggests that matter has the capacity to store information. Similarly, studies in environmental psychology highlight how the emotional resonance of a space affects those who enter it. Although these insights do not fully explain residual energy, they align with the ancient understanding that places and objects are more than inert; they are vessels of memory.

Residual energy is created through intense emotional experiences, repeated actions, or significant events. A joyous celebration, a prolonged period of anxiety, or a sudden act of violence can leave distinct energetic signatures. Over time, these imprints may fade or integrate into the surrounding energy field, but in some cases, they persist, forming a subtle layer of history that influences the present.

The ability to sense residual energy varies among individuals. Some may feel a room's "vibe" upon entering, experiencing warmth or unease without understanding why. Others may perceive these energies more vividly, describing them as sensations, images, or even auditory impressions. Such sensitivity can be developed through practice, but it requires a mindful approach to avoid becoming overwhelmed by the energetic residues of others.

Practical methods for assessing residual energy begin with observation. Quiet the mind and tune into the subtle sensations of a space. Does it feel welcoming or heavy? Are there areas that seem particularly vibrant or stagnant? Paying attention to temperature shifts, bodily reactions, and intuitive impressions provides valuable clues about the energetic history of a place or object.

Once identified, residual energy can be worked with intentionally. Cleansing rituals are a time-honored practice for transforming or neutralizing dense energies. Smoke from sacred plants, such as sage or palo santo, is commonly used to purify spaces, while sound—bells, singing bowls, or mantras—breaks up stagnant vibrations. Light, particularly sunlight or candlelight, is another powerful tool for clearing energetic residues.

Objects, too, carry energetic imprints. Jewelry, heirlooms, and artifacts often absorb the emotions and intentions of their creators and owners. Psychometry, the ability to sense the history of an object through touch, offers insights into these energetic layers. Holding an item and meditating on its vibrations can reveal its story, but it also requires discernment to separate personal projections from genuine impressions.

In cases where residual energy feels oppressive or intrusive, stronger measures may be needed. Salt, both physical and energetic, has long been revered for its cleansing properties.

Sprinkling salt around a space, placing it in corners, or dissolving it in water for cleaning can dispel unwanted energies. Similarly, grounding practices—such as connecting with the earth through barefoot walking or visualization—help release accumulated energies and restore balance.

Not all residual energy is negative or in need of removal. Sacred spaces, for instance, are often intentionally imbued with positive energy to create an atmosphere conducive to meditation, healing, or worship. Preserving and amplifying such energies involves regular care, including rituals, offerings, and maintaining an attitude of reverence.

As one deepens their understanding of residual energy, the concept of "energetic hygiene" becomes paramount. Just as physical cleanliness is essential for health, so too is the regular cleansing of one's energetic field. Practices such as visualization, energy baths, or the use of protective crystals help maintain clarity and prevent the absorption of external residues.

The ethical considerations of working with residual energy cannot be overlooked. Spaces and objects hold memories that are not ours to claim or alter without respect. Approaching this work with humility and an intention to heal ensures that interactions with residual energy honor its origins and contribute to harmony.

There is also a collective dimension to residual energy. Cities, nations, and even the Earth itself carry the imprints of human actions. Sites of historical trauma, such as former battlefields or areas affected by natural disasters, resonate with the echoes of their past. Healing these energies requires both individual and collective efforts. Ceremonies, prayers, and acts of remembrance serve to acknowledge the past and transmute its lingering effects.

The Earth's natural features also play a role in residual energy. Mountains, rivers, and forests act as anchors for energy, absorbing and redistributing it across the landscape. Sacred sites, marked by unique geological formations or energetic qualities, amplify the flow of energy, serving as reservoirs of vitality and inspiration. Recognizing and respecting these natural energy centers enhances one's connection to the web of life.

Ultimately, the study of residual energy is a journey into the layers of existence that transcend the physical. It reveals the interconnectedness of all things and the enduring impact of our thoughts, emotions, and actions. By working consciously with residual energy, we become stewards of the unseen, capable of transforming the past's echoes into a harmonious foundation for the present and future.

To honor residual energy is to honor the stories it carries, both the struggles and triumphs that define the human experience. By attuning to these subtle imprints, we gain insight into the invisible forces that shape our world, fostering a deeper understanding of the energetic tapestry in which we are all entwined.

Chapter 43
Inner Cycles

Life, in all its complexity, unfolds through patterns as ancient as the stars and as intimate as a heartbeat. Inner cycles govern the rhythms of our existence, echoing the cosmic dances of planets and the subtle pulses of the Earth. These cycles are not arbitrary; they are the scaffolding upon which physical, emotional, and spiritual experiences are constructed. By exploring the interplay of these cycles within ourselves, we uncover profound connections to the greater tapestry of existence.

Inner cycles are evident in the natural world. The tides rise and fall, the moon waxes and wanes, and the seasons shift in predictable yet infinitely variable patterns. Humanity, inseparable from this rhythm, reflects these movements in myriad ways. Biorhythms, circadian cycles, and hormonal fluctuations mirror the intricate choreography of universal forces, anchoring us to the flow of time.

The human body is a masterpiece of cyclical patterns. From the steady rhythm of the heart to the expansive process of breath, each function depends on the balance of recurring processes. Cellular regeneration, digestion, and even thought processes align with cycles, some rapid and fleeting, others slow and profound. These physiological rhythms form the foundation of our energetic field, resonating with both our internal and external environments.

Emotional and mental cycles weave another layer into this dynamic structure. Moods, memories, and mental clarity ebb and flow like currents, influenced by factors both within and beyond our control. Recognizing these patterns reveals opportunities for growth and transformation. For instance, times of introspection often follow periods of heightened activity, allowing for integration and renewal. This interplay, when consciously observed, offers a deeper understanding of our inner landscape.

Ancient traditions understood the significance of inner cycles and developed practices to align with them. Vedic astrology, for example, correlates planetary movements with personal growth phases, while Chinese medicine emphasizes the flow of qi through meridians in daily and seasonal cycles. Indigenous wisdom, rooted in the rhythms of the Earth, teaches that humanity thrives when in harmony with the natural world's cadence.

In the modern world, many have become disconnected from these cycles. Artificial lighting, constant digital stimulation, and an ever-accelerating pace of life obscure the subtle cues that once guided human activity. This disconnection leads to imbalance, manifesting as stress, fatigue, and a diminished sense of purpose. Reclaiming awareness of inner cycles is not merely a return to an ancient practice—it is a pathway to healing and renewal.

The first step in attuning to inner cycles is observation. Begin by noting daily rhythms—when energy peaks and wanes, how emotions shift with the time of day, and how external factors influence these patterns. Journaling provides a tangible way to track these observations over time, revealing recurring themes and tendencies. Such awareness forms the foundation for deeper exploration.

Meditation serves as a powerful tool for tuning into inner cycles. By quieting the mind, one can sense the subtle currents that shape thoughts and emotions. Techniques focusing on the breath—its rhythm and depth—offer a direct connection to these cycles. With practice, meditation becomes a mirror reflecting the dynamic balance of internal forces.

Seasonal cycles, though external, have profound effects on the inner world. The introspective energy of winter, the renewal of spring, the vitality of summer, and the release of autumn each correspond to specific phases of personal growth. Engaging with these energies enhances alignment with the natural flow of life. Simple practices, such as observing seasonal changes in diet or incorporating rituals aligned with the seasons, deepen this connection.

Dreams are another portal into the understanding of inner cycles. Dream patterns often reflect unresolved emotions or insights emerging from the subconscious. By paying attention to recurring dream themes, one can discern cycles of growth and transformation. Practices such as dream journaling and lucid dreaming techniques enhance awareness of these nocturnal rhythms.

The interplay between inner and outer cycles extends to relationships. Connections with others follow rhythms of their own—periods of closeness and distance, harmony and challenge. Recognizing these patterns fosters understanding and compassion, allowing for greater depth in interpersonal dynamics. This awareness also extends to group energies, where collective cycles influence communities and organizations.

One of the most profound inner cycles is the soul's journey through life. Ancient traditions describe this cycle in terms of spiritual growth, with phases of learning, integration, and transcendence. Astrology, numerology, and similar systems offer frameworks for understanding these phases, providing insights into the broader purpose and direction of one's life.

Practical techniques for aligning with inner cycles include mindfulness practices, rhythmic movement, and intentional rest. Yoga and tai chi synchronize breath and movement, harmonizing the physical and energetic bodies. Journaling serves as a reflective practice, capturing the essence of cyclical experiences and revealing patterns over time. Fasting, when practiced mindfully, can reset physiological cycles and offer clarity on an energetic level.

Working with lunar cycles offers another pathway to understanding inner rhythms. The new moon invites intention-setting, while the waxing phase builds momentum. The full moon amplifies energy, making it a powerful time for reflection and manifestation, and the waning moon encourages release and rest. Aligning practices with these phases enhances their efficacy and deepens one's connection to natural cycles.

Balance is the essence of navigating inner cycles. Just as the moon's phases are neither static nor random, so too must one flow with the shifts of inner rhythms. Resistance to these changes creates tension, while acceptance fosters harmony. Practices that ground the body and calm the mind, such as grounding exercises or nature walks, provide stability amidst the dynamic flux of inner cycles.

Exploring inner cycles is a journey into the heart of existence itself. These rhythms, though invisible, shape every aspect of life, connecting the personal with the cosmic. As one learns to align with these cycles, a sense of ease and clarity emerges, revealing the profound intelligence underlying all of creation.

To honor inner cycles is to honor the sacred rhythm of life. It is an invitation to live in harmony with the unseen forces that sustain and guide us, to embrace change as an opportunity for growth, and to celebrate the beauty of life's infinite patterns. Through this awareness, one becomes not merely an observer but an active participant in the great dance of existence.

Chapter 44
A New Horizon

The horizon has always symbolized a boundary, a line separating the known from the unknown. Yet, as one approaches it, the horizon shifts, beckoning further exploration. Humanity's journey mirrors this phenomenon, a constant movement toward understanding deeper truths and expanding the limits of perception. Energetic emanations, the unseen currents that shape existence, now invite us to step beyond familiar boundaries and into a new era of conscious evolution.

This new horizon is not a distant destination—it is already present, woven into the fabric of daily life. It emerges as the collective awareness of subtle energies grows, transforming individual and societal paradigms. This chapter examines the dynamics of this evolutionary shift, exploring how emanations guide humanity's progress and how conscious engagement with these energies can shape a future of harmony and interconnectedness.

Throughout history, periods of transformation have often been preceded by disruptions—upheavals that challenge old structures and create space for new growth. These moments act as thresholds, where the energies of the past converge with the potential of the future. Humanity stands at such a threshold now, facing crises of ecology, technology, and identity. Beneath these challenges, however, lies an unprecedented opportunity to align with higher frequencies of emanation and co-create a more harmonious reality.

The currents of evolution are not abstract; they manifest through individual and collective experiences. Each person carries within them a unique energetic signature, contributing to the greater field of human consciousness. When individuals attune to their inner energies and align with universal principles, they amplify this collective field, influencing the trajectory of human evolution.

One of the key dynamics of this new horizon is the convergence of ancient wisdom and modern science. Long-separated domains are finding resonance, as quantum physics validates concepts that mystics and sages have articulated for millennia. Nonlocality, entanglement, and the interconnected nature of the universe mirror teachings about the web of life and the unity of existence. This synthesis of knowledge catalyzes a deeper understanding of emanations and their role in shaping reality.

Technology, often perceived as a force of separation, holds the potential to bridge gaps and amplify the collective consciousness. Innovations in communication and data-sharing enable the rapid dissemination of ideas, creating networks of individuals united by shared intentions. Technologies that measure subtle energies, such as biofeedback and energy-mapping tools, provide tangible ways to explore emanations and their effects. However, technology must be guided by wisdom to serve as a tool for elevation rather than disconnection.

Communities play a vital role in anchoring the energies of the new horizon. Groups united by shared purpose create powerful energetic fields, amplifying intentions and fostering transformation. Spiritual gatherings, collective meditations, and intentional communities act as nodes in a global web of energy, each contributing to the emergence of a more harmonious collective consciousness. These spaces provide opportunities for individuals to deepen their connection to emanations and explore their potential for healing and creation.

The Earth itself is a partner in this evolutionary process. Its energetic systems, from geomagnetic fields to ley lines, interact with human consciousness, providing support and guidance. Sacred sites, where the Earth's energies are particularly strong, serve as portals for transformation, offering unique opportunities to connect with higher frequencies. By aligning with the Earth's rhythms and honoring its wisdom, humanity can harmonize with the larger cycles of planetary evolution.

Practical tools for engaging with the energies of this new horizon include meditation, visualization, and intentional action. Meditation quiets the mind, creating a receptive space for subtle energies to emerge. Visualization harnesses the power of imagination to shape reality, translating energetic intentions into physical manifestations. Intentional action grounds these practices in the material world, bridging the gap between vision and reality.

Collective practices amplify the power of individual efforts. Group meditations, synchronized across time and space, create resonant fields that transcend physical boundaries. Rituals celebrating solstices, equinoxes, and other natural cycles align participants with the rhythms of the cosmos. Acts of service, grounded in compassion and unity, ripple outward, infusing the collective field with higher vibrations.

Education and awareness are essential components of this evolutionary shift. As more individuals understand the nature of emanations and their role in shaping reality, they become empowered to navigate this new landscape. Integrating teachings about energy into educational systems, healthcare, and community practices ensures that future generations are equipped to engage consciously with these dynamics.

The new horizon also invites us to reconsider the nature of leadership. In this emerging paradigm, leadership is not about control or hierarchy but about alignment and resonance. True leaders act as energetic anchors, embodying the qualities they wish to inspire in others. They guide not through force but through the coherence of their presence, creating spaces where others can awaken to their own potential.

Challenges are inevitable on this journey, as old patterns resist dissolution and new paradigms take root. Fear, division, and resistance are natural responses to change, but they are also opportunities for growth. By recognizing these energies as part of the evolutionary process, individuals and communities can transform them into catalysts for deeper alignment.

A key practice in navigating this new horizon is cultivating resilience—the ability to adapt and thrive amidst change. Resilience arises from a strong connection to one's inner essence, the unchanging core that remains steady amidst life's fluctuations. Practices such as grounding, breathwork, and self-reflection strengthen this connection, enabling individuals to move through challenges with grace and clarity.

The journey toward the new horizon is not linear. It is a spiral, a process of revisiting and deepening understanding at each turn. Moments of insight alternate with periods of integration, as the energies of the past are transmuted into the foundation for the future. This rhythm mirrors the cycles of nature, reminding us that evolution is not about arrival but about continuous unfolding.

As humanity steps into this new horizon, the role of emanations becomes increasingly clear. They are the threads that connect the personal with the universal, the visible with the invisible, the known with the infinite potential of the unknown. By attuning to these energies, individuals and communities become co-creators of a reality grounded in harmony, wisdom, and love.

The horizon may forever remain just beyond reach, but it is not a limitation—it is an invitation. It calls us to expand our vision, deepen our connection, and embrace the infinite possibilities of existence. In answering this call, we discover that the journey itself is the destination, a dance of energies that reveals the profound unity of all life.

Chapter 45
Spiritual Pathways

The labyrinth of spiritual traditions that spans humanity's history is not a maze of disconnection but a network of converging streams, each pathway an expression of the universal quest for truth. Across cultures and epochs, these spiritual pathways have provided frameworks for engaging with emanations—the vital energies that shape existence—and for cultivating a deeper relationship with the unseen forces that permeate the cosmos.

This chapter explores the diversity of spiritual traditions, their unique practices, and the shared principles that underpin their approaches to emanations. It examines the tools these traditions offer for navigating the inner and outer dimensions of existence, guiding individuals toward a greater alignment with the universal energy flow. At its core, this chapter reveals how the multiplicity of spiritual paths ultimately converges in the experience of unity with the whole.

From the ancient shamans who danced in trance to the hymns of celestial order sung in Vedic temples, each tradition has served as a bridge between the material and the spiritual. Shamanic traditions, among the earliest pathways to spiritual understanding, viewed emanations as the threads of life itself. Shamans acted as weavers of these threads, journeying into altered states of consciousness to restore harmony to the energetic fabric of their communities. Through rituals, chants, and the use of sacred plants, they accessed realms of pure energy, returning with insights to heal, guide, and transform.

The Vedic tradition, with its intricate cosmology, developed profound systems for understanding emanations. The concept of **prana**, the life force, is central to practices such as yoga and pranayama, where the breath becomes the key to harnessing and directing energy. The chakras—energetic centers within the body—are explored in detail, offering practitioners a map for balancing internal emanations. By aligning these centers, individuals awaken latent energies and achieve a harmonious state that mirrors the universal rhythm.

Mystical traditions in Abrahamic faiths also reveal profound engagement with emanations. In Kabbalistic teachings, the **sefirot** represent emanations of divine energy, mapping the flow from the infinite to the finite. Each sefirah embodies a specific quality—wisdom, beauty, strength—guiding practitioners in their quest to embody divine attributes. Sufi mystics, through their ecstatic dances and poetic verses, transcend the boundaries of the self, merging with the infinite through the whirling energy of devotion.

Indigenous practices around the world demonstrate a profound attunement to the Earth's emanations. Native American ceremonies honor the interconnectedness of life through rituals that align with natural cycles. The use of drums and chants in these traditions serves not only as an expression of reverence but as a method for harmonizing with the Earth's vibrations. Similarly, the Aboriginal concept of the Dreamtime connects individuals to the ancestral emanations that sustain creation, reminding them of their role as stewards of this intricate web of life.

Despite their cultural differences, these traditions share underlying principles: reverence for the unseen forces, practices for attunement, and a commitment to personal and collective transformation. They each emphasize the importance of cultivating awareness of emanations, teaching that the flow of energy can be harnessed for healing, creation, and transcendence.

The tools provided by these traditions are as diverse as the traditions themselves. Meditation, prayer, chanting, visualization, and movement are all methods for aligning with subtle energies. Meditation, in particular, transcends cultural boundaries, offering a direct means to quiet the mind and perceive the underlying current of emanations. Whether practiced in the stillness of Zen or the devotional focus of Christian mysticism, meditation opens the gateway to deeper states of awareness.

Prayer, often misunderstood as a mere act of supplication, is another universal tool. At its core, prayer is an alignment of intention with the higher frequencies of emanations. In its many forms—mantras, affirmations, or spontaneous expressions—prayer acts as a channel through which the practitioner attunes to the flow of universal energy. Chanting amplifies this process, using sound as a vehicle to harmonize internal and external vibrations.

Movement-based practices, such as Tai Chi, Qi Gong, and sacred dance, integrate the physical body with the energetic field, creating a seamless flow of energy. These practices demonstrate that spiritual pathways are not confined to stillness but extend into the dynamic interplay of motion and energy. The body becomes a vessel for the divine, expressing emanations through every movement.

As seekers traverse these pathways, discernment becomes essential. The abundance of spiritual teachings can overwhelm or mislead, particularly in a modern context where traditions are often diluted or commercialized. True discernment arises not from intellectual analysis but from resonance—a felt sense of alignment with a particular practice or teaching. The energy of a tradition must harmonize with the seeker's inner frequency, creating a mutual amplification that propels the journey forward.

Challenges are inevitable on the spiritual path. Doubt, distraction, and resistance arise as the ego struggles to maintain control amidst the transformative power of emanations. Yet, these challenges are not obstacles but opportunities for growth. Each moment of difficulty invites deeper surrender to the flow of energy, revealing hidden layers of self and expanding awareness.

Integration is the final step on the spiritual pathway. The goal is not to escape the material world but to bring the wisdom of emanations into every aspect of life. Daily practices, no matter how simple, become acts of alignment. Eating, walking, speaking—all are infused with the awareness of energy, transforming the mundane into the sacred. This integration is the essence of spiritual mastery: to live as a bridge between the seen and unseen, embodying the unity of existence.

The spiritual pathways explored in this chapter remind us that the journey is not about choosing the "right" tradition but about embracing the one that resonates most deeply. Each path offers unique gifts, yet all lead to the same destination: the realization that we are not separate from the emanations that shape reality but integral expressions of their infinite flow.

As humanity continues its collective journey toward the new horizon, these pathways will serve as vital guides. They offer not only wisdom but also practical tools for navigating the energetic shifts of this era. By walking these paths with awareness and openness, individuals contribute to the elevation of the collective field, co-creating a future grounded in harmony and connection.

In the end, the spiritual pathway is not a linear progression but a spiral journey, continually deepening and expanding. It invites us to return to the same truths with greater clarity, to see the unity within diversity, and to recognize that the path itself is the destination. Through these pathways, we awaken to the profound mystery of existence, embracing the endless dance of emanations that sustains all life.

Chapter 46
Conscious Prosperity

Conscious prosperity arises not from the mere accumulation of material wealth but from the harmonious flow of energy that aligns one's spiritual purpose with the physical world. Prosperity, at its essence, is an energetic state—a reflection of balance between giving and receiving, intention and manifestation. This chapter delves into the profound connection between emanations and abundance, exploring how conscious engagement with universal energies can create a foundation for sustainable prosperity that transcends materialism.

Across cultures, the concept of abundance has often been intertwined with spiritual practices and beliefs. Ancient traditions viewed wealth not merely as a collection of resources but as a symbol of alignment with the divine flow. In Egyptian cosmology, Ma'at represented balance and order, including the responsible stewardship of prosperity. Similarly, Vedic teachings saw material abundance as a reflection of **Lakshmi's** blessings, linked to righteousness and harmony with universal dharma.

At the heart of conscious prosperity lies intention. Every thought, word, and action carries an energetic frequency that shapes reality. Intentions act as seeds within the energetic field, influencing how resources flow into one's life. Setting clear, aligned intentions creates coherence within one's energy field, enabling an unhindered exchange with the universe. Without this alignment, prosperity often becomes fleeting, leaving individuals in cycles of scarcity or imbalance.

Practical techniques for cultivating prosperity begin with an inner audit of one's beliefs and emotions surrounding wealth.

Limiting beliefs, often rooted in ancestral patterns or cultural conditioning, block the flow of abundance. These beliefs manifest as energetic distortions, creating resistance to receiving. Practices such as guided visualization, affirmations, and energy clearing rituals help dismantle these blocks, creating space for new patterns to emerge.

Visualization is particularly powerful in activating the energy of prosperity. When one envisions abundance with clarity and emotional resonance, the subconscious mind aligns with this reality. Combining visualization with specific actions amplifies its effect, anchoring the energetic intention in the physical realm. Rituals that honor cycles of gratitude and giving further reinforce this alignment, creating a dynamic exchange with the universal field.

Energy flows where attention goes. This principle underscores the importance of focus in manifesting conscious prosperity. Dispersed energy—through worry, distraction, or fear—creates fragmentation, while focused energy becomes a magnet for abundance. Practices such as meditation, journaling, and breathwork cultivate the presence necessary to direct attention intentionally, ensuring that one's energetic output aligns with their desired outcomes.

The role of gratitude cannot be overstated in the cultivation of conscious prosperity. Gratitude acts as an amplifier, magnifying the energy of abundance already present. By expressing genuine appreciation for the resources, opportunities, and relationships in one's life, individuals open pathways for greater prosperity to flow. Gratitude ceremonies, whether performed alone or within community, create energetic coherence, enhancing the overall frequency of the individual or group.

Sustainability is a vital component of conscious prosperity. In many indigenous cultures, wealth was measured not by accumulation but by the well-being of the community and the environment. Prosperity was a shared experience, with resources circulated to ensure balance. Modern practices can draw from these principles, emphasizing ethical consumption, fair exchange, and the reinvestment of resources into causes that uplift others and the planet.

Money, as a manifestation of energy, carries its own vibrational imprint. The way one earns, spends, and shares money reflects their relationship with this energy. Conscious engagement with money transforms it from a source of stress or greed into a tool for empowerment and healing. Financial rituals, such as blessing one's income or creating sacred spaces for financial decision-making, imbue this process with intention and mindfulness.

However, conscious prosperity extends beyond individual gain. Collective abundance arises when communities align their energies to support shared visions. The pooling of resources—whether through collaborative projects, shared economies, or philanthropic efforts—creates an expansive field of prosperity that benefits all participants. This reciprocity mirrors the natural cycles of the Earth, where abundance thrives through interconnected systems.

Challenges on the path to conscious prosperity often stem from fear—fear of lack, fear of failure, or fear of unworthiness. These fears disrupt the energetic flow, creating scarcity consciousness. Overcoming these fears requires deep inner work, often through shadow exploration and the healing of unresolved emotional wounds. Practices such as energy healing, journaling, or working with spiritual mentors help address these fears, restoring trust in the flow of abundance.

The intersection of spirituality and material wealth raises profound ethical questions. How can one pursue prosperity without succumbing to materialism? How does one balance personal desires with the greater good? The answer lies in intention and alignment. Prosperity that arises from a place of service, integrity, and connection to the whole becomes a force for transformation. It uplifts not only the individual but also the collective, creating ripples of positive change.

Integration is key to sustaining conscious prosperity. This involves weaving the principles of alignment, gratitude, and ethical action into everyday life. Small, consistent practices—such as blessing meals, setting daily intentions, or celebrating milestones—anchor these principles, ensuring that prosperity remains grounded and sustainable. Regular reflection on one's values and goals keeps the journey aligned with a deeper purpose.

The chapter concludes with advanced techniques for enhancing prosperity through subtle energy work. Practices such as working with crystal grids, invoking elemental energies, or creating abundance altars deepen the connection between physical and spiritual abundance. These rituals not only attract resources but also cultivate a state of inner richness, where prosperity becomes a natural extension of one's being.

Ultimately, conscious prosperity is not an endpoint but a journey—a dynamic interplay between giving and receiving, intention and manifestation. It calls individuals to step beyond the illusion of separation, recognizing that true abundance flows when one's actions align with the greater harmony of the universe. Through this alignment, prosperity becomes not merely a personal gain but a shared experience, enriching the collective fabric of existence.

Chapter 47
Inner Flame

The inner flame is the primordial spark of existence, a radiant force that resides within every being. It is the essence of life, the unyielding ember that bridges the finite with the infinite. This chapter explores the nature of the inner flame, its relationship with emanations, and the profound journey of nurturing it toward enlightenment. By understanding and working with this luminous force, individuals can awaken their highest potential and align their lives with the universal flow.

The inner flame has been symbolized across cultures and spiritual traditions, from the eternal fire of Zoroastrianism to the divine spark described in Gnostic teachings. In Vedic philosophy, it is represented by **Agni**, the sacred fire that mediates between humanity and the cosmos. In alchemical texts, this flame is the **ignis internus**, the transformative fire that purifies and elevates. These symbols converge on the recognition of the inner flame as both a source of illumination and a tool for transmutation.

This flame is not static; it flickers and shifts in response to one's inner and outer states. When nurtured, it burns brightly, providing clarity, vitality, and purpose. When neglected, it dims, leaving the individual disconnected from their essence. The path to tending the inner flame begins with awareness—recognizing its presence and understanding the conditions that fuel or dampen its glow.

Breath is one of the primary tools for connecting with the inner flame. In many spiritual practices, breath is seen as the carrier of life force, capable of stoking the flame into a steady blaze. Rhythmic breathing exercises, such as those found in pranayama or qigong, create a bridge between the physical and subtle bodies, feeding the inner fire. Each inhalation becomes an act of kindling, each exhalation a release of what no longer serves.

Meditation is another key practice for tending the flame. In stillness, the layers of distraction and resistance that obscure the inner light begin to dissolve. Visualization techniques, such as envisioning a golden flame within the heart or at the base of the spine, help focus attention on this luminous center. With regular practice, this visualization evolves into a direct experience, where the flame is felt as a tangible presence, radiating warmth and energy.

The inner flame thrives on alignment—alignment with truth, intention, and the natural flow of energy. Actions and thoughts that resonate with one's authentic self feed the flame, while those that create dissonance diminish it. This principle underscores the importance of integrity in one's spiritual and everyday life. Aligning with the inner flame involves continuous self-inquiry, asking: **Does this choice honor my true essence?** When the answer is yes, the flame responds with renewed strength.

Emotion is another powerful influence on the flame. Joy, love, and gratitude serve as fuel, amplifying its radiance. Conversely, unresolved anger, fear, or shame act as dampers, smothering the flame under layers of dense energy. The work of releasing these emotions is not merely therapeutic but transformative, as it clears the pathways for the flame to shine unobstructed. Practices such as journaling, energy healing, or sacred rituals provide tools for this emotional alchemy.

The concept of the inner flame extends beyond the individual. In relationships, it manifests as the spark of connection, the shared energy that binds people in mutual understanding and support. Recognizing and honoring the flame in others deepens these connections, creating a shared field of light. Community rituals, collective meditations, and shared acts of service amplify this communal flame, weaving individual energies into a collective blaze.

The journey of the inner flame is also marked by phases of challenge and transformation. There are moments when the flame may appear to dim or even extinguish—times of loss, confusion, or spiritual crisis. Yet these dark nights of the soul often serve as catalysts for profound growth. In the ashes of these trials, the flame is rekindled, often stronger and more resilient than before. This cycle of death and rebirth mirrors the alchemical process, where the base material is dissolved and purified to reveal its golden essence.

Sacred symbols and tools can serve as allies in this journey. Candles, for example, are a tangible representation of the inner flame, and lighting them during meditation or ritual creates a physical and energetic connection to this inner light. Crystals like citrine or sunstone resonate with the energy of the flame, amplifying its warmth and vitality. Mantras, such as those invoking divine fire, carry vibrations that stoke the flame and align it with higher frequencies.

As the inner flame grows, it becomes a beacon—not only illuminating one's path but also radiating outward to inspire and guide others. This outward flow of light reflects the universal law of emanation: that which is cultivated within naturally extends beyond. The flame, once perceived as a personal force, is revealed to be a manifestation of the universal fire, connecting all beings in an eternal dance of light.

The chapter culminates with advanced practices for merging with the inner flame. These include breath of fire techniques, where rapid breathing ignites intense energetic activation; meditations on the sun as a cosmic flame, drawing its energy into the body; and heart-focused practices that expand the flame's radiance beyond the physical self. These practices are not ends in themselves but doorways to a profound state of being, where the boundary between the individual flame and the universal fire dissolves.

Ultimately, the journey with the inner flame is a return to the self—to the unchanging essence that has always been present. It is a reminder that enlightenment is not a distant goal but an ever-present potential, waiting to be kindled. By tending this flame with care, intention, and love, one steps into their fullest expression, becoming both a vessel and a source of light in the infinite web of existence.

Chapter 48
Final Harmony

Final harmony is the culmination of the journey through emanations, the point where the threads of all practices, insights, and transformations weave into a cohesive whole. It is not an ending but a convergence—a state of equilibrium where the individual vibrates in resonance with the universal rhythm. This chapter explores the nature of harmony as both an internal and external phenomenon and offers pathways to integrate and sustain it within the flow of life.

Harmony begins within, as a delicate balance of energies across the physical, emotional, mental, and spiritual dimensions. The subtle bodies, which often operate in isolation or discord, must be brought into alignment. Each body represents a layer of existence, vibrating at its unique frequency, and the interplay between them creates the symphony of the self. When these frequencies resonate coherently, the inner being becomes a conduit for universal energies, reflecting the cosmic order.

This alignment begins with awareness—a precise attunement to the state of each dimension. The physical body speaks through sensations, the emotional body through feelings, the mental body through thoughts, and the spiritual body through intuition and presence. Practices such as body scans, emotional journaling, mindfulness meditation, and intuitive inquiry allow for the identification of imbalances. Once revealed, these can be gently harmonized through targeted techniques.

Breathwork is central to establishing this equilibrium. The breath acts as a bridge, moving between dimensions and carrying vitality into areas of stagnation. Rhythmic breathing practices, particularly those emphasizing diaphragmatic and elongated exhales, create coherence in the nervous system and establish a foundation of inner calm. This state of coherence amplifies the natural capacity for self-regulation, allowing the body and mind to recalibrate.

Sound and vibration also play a vital role in achieving harmony. From ancient chants to modern sound baths, the intentional use of frequencies creates shifts in energy fields, dissolving discord and restoring resonance. Singing bowls, gongs, and voice toning can be integrated into personal practices to align with specific frequencies associated with healing and integration. The mantra **AUM**, believed to encapsulate the primordial sound of creation, holds particular power in unifying fragmented energies.

Movement deepens this alignment, as conscious physicality brings the inner and outer worlds into harmony. Practices such as tai chi, qigong, and ecstatic dance activate energy flows while grounding the individual in the present moment. These movements are not merely exercises but expressions of the universal rhythm, allowing one to participate in the dance of life with intention and grace. Even simple, mindful walks in nature can serve as powerful harmonizing rituals.

As internal harmony is cultivated, it naturally radiates outward. Relationships, once strained by misunderstandings and energetic imbalances, transform under the light of resonance. The practice of conscious communication becomes a means of sustaining this harmony, emphasizing presence, empathy, and authenticity. Energetic boundaries, maintained with clarity and compassion, ensure that this resonance is not disrupted by external discord.

Harmony with the environment is equally essential. Ancient practices of feng shui, geomancy, and space clearing teach how to align living spaces with the natural flow of energy. These principles, grounded in observation of the elemental forces, offer tools to harmonize with the earth's vibrations. Clearing clutter, using intentional lighting, and incorporating natural materials create an environment that supports inner equilibrium.

The path to final harmony also involves embracing the cyclical nature of existence. Just as the seasons flow from one to the next, so too does the human experience oscillate between phases of growth, rest, and renewal. Resistance to these cycles creates friction, while acceptance allows for fluidity. Rituals that honor these transitions, such as solstice meditations or personal reflections at the new moon, foster an understanding of one's place within the greater cycles of life.

One of the greatest barriers to harmony is the illusion of separation—between self and others, matter and spirit, or the individual and the universal. Practices that dissolve these boundaries, such as non-dual meditation or contemplations on interbeing, reveal the interconnectedness of all things. The realization of this unity is not merely intellectual but a lived experience, where the self is felt as an inseparable part of the whole.

Final harmony is also an act of service. By living in alignment, one becomes a beacon, amplifying coherence within their community and the wider world. Collective meditations, group rituals, and acts of kindness ripple outward, strengthening the web of life. The concept of morphic resonance suggests that as more individuals achieve harmony, the collective consciousness is elevated, making it easier for others to follow the same path.

Symbolically, final harmony is often represented by the mandala, a sacred geometric form that encapsulates balance and unity. Creating or meditating on a mandala allows the mind to align with these principles, integrating the diverse elements of existence into a centered whole. These forms can also serve as personal or communal tools for setting intentions, reflecting the inner journey onto the external canvas.

The advanced practices of final harmony involve simultaneous engagement with multiple dimensions. For example, a session might begin with grounding exercises, progress to breathwork and sound healing, and conclude with a meditative visualization of unity. These layered practices amplify the harmonizing effects, creating a holistic resonance that permeates the being.

Ultimately, final harmony is not a static state but a dynamic interplay—a dance with the ever-changing flows of life. It requires vigilance, adaptability, and an unwavering commitment to alignment. Each moment becomes an opportunity to refine this resonance, to tune the instrument of the self to the symphony of the cosmos.

In the pursuit of final harmony, the individual transcends the illusion of fragmentation and steps into the truth of wholeness. Life is no longer a series of disconnected events but a seamless expression of the universal rhythm. By living in this state, one becomes both a witness and a participant in the great unfolding, embodying the timeless truth that all emanations converge in harmony.

Chapter 49
Return to the Whole

As the journey of emanations reaches its final chapter, the concept of wholeness emerges not as a destination but as the essence of existence itself. This chapter is an exploration of unity—a transcendence of duality, where individual and universal, seen and unseen, form and formlessness dissolve into a singular, infinite continuum. The return to the whole is not a process of becoming but of remembering, a realization of what has always been.

Wholeness is an intrinsic state, veiled only by the illusions of separation that permeate human perception. This chapter begins by addressing these illusions, tracing their origins in the fragmentation of consciousness. The mind, in its effort to categorize and understand, creates divisions—between self and other, matter and energy, time and eternity. While these divisions serve practical purposes, they obscure the deeper truth of interconnectedness.

The path to wholeness lies in dismantling these artificial boundaries. Ancient spiritual traditions, quantum physics, and transpersonal psychology all converge on the understanding that separation is a construct. At the quantum level, particles are entangled, their states inseparable across vast distances. In the spiritual realm, the mystic's insight affirms that all beings are facets of the same divine essence. These perspectives offer not only validation but a roadmap for experiencing unity.

Central to this experience is the dissolution of ego—a relinquishment of the constructed self. The ego, with its incessant need for identity and distinction, clings to separateness as a defense against the vastness of the whole. Practices of self-inquiry, such as the Advaitic question "Who am I?", expose the ego's illusory nature. As the layers of identity peel away, what remains is pure awareness—boundless, eternal, and indivisible.

Meditation is a powerful gateway to this state. Techniques such as open awareness meditation or Dzogchen's "resting in the natural state" allow the practitioner to perceive the seamless flow of existence. In these moments, the boundaries between observer and observed dissolve, and the unity of all things becomes palpable. The realization of this unity is often accompanied by profound peace, as the individual recognizes their place within the cosmic order.

The return to the whole also involves an embrace of paradox. Light and shadow, creation and destruction, order and chaos—these apparent opposites are revealed as complementary aspects of a singular force. This understanding is not abstract but deeply practical. It allows one to navigate the complexities of life with grace, accepting the ebb and flow of existence as expressions of the same underlying reality.

Symbols of wholeness, such as the circle, spiral, and infinity loop, offer profound insights into this truth. These forms, recurring in nature and sacred art, encapsulate the cyclical and interconnected nature of life. Contemplating these symbols, whether through art, visualization, or ritual, awakens a visceral sense of unity. Mandalas, in particular, serve as mirrors of the universe, inviting the observer to step into the center and perceive the harmony of the whole.

Wholeness is also reflected in the natural world. The ecosystem, with its intricate web of relationships, is a living testament to the interdependence of all life. Observing nature, whether through the flight of birds, the growth of trees, or the flow of water, reveals the seamless interconnection of all things. Practices such as forest bathing, stargazing, or simply sitting in silence with the earth provide profound reminders of this truth.

Returning to the whole does not mean abandoning individuality but transcending its limitations. The individual self, once seen as separate, is now recognized as a unique expression of the universal. This shift transforms the way one engages with life. Actions are no longer driven by fear or scarcity but by the joy of participation in a greater symphony. Relationships become opportunities for connection rather than conflict, as the self sees its reflection in others.

One of the profound realizations of wholeness is the timelessness of existence. Linear time, with its divisions of past, present, and future, gives way to the eternal now—a dimension where all moments coexist. This understanding reshapes the way one perceives life's transitions, such as birth and death. These are no longer seen as beginnings and endings but as transformations within the infinite flow of being.

The practice of gratitude emerges as a natural expression of wholeness. Recognizing the interconnectedness of all things, one feels a deep appreciation for every experience, person, and moment. Gratitude becomes not just an emotion but a state of being, a way of affirming the abundance inherent in life. This attitude opens the heart, creating a feedback loop of positivity that resonates with the world.

Wholeness also calls for service—a sharing of the gifts discovered on the journey. This service is not an obligation but a spontaneous act arising from the realization that helping others is, in essence, helping oneself. Whether through teaching, healing, creating, or simply being present, acts of service amplify the energy of unity. They ripple outward, touching lives and inspiring others to embark on their own journeys of return.

The chapter concludes with the practice of surrender—not as a loss of agency but as the ultimate act of trust. Surrendering to the flow of life, one aligns with the greater intelligence that governs the universe. This surrender is not passive but dynamic, requiring attunement and responsiveness to the present moment. It is the recognition that the self is both a drop in the ocean and the ocean itself.

The return to the whole is not a finale but an ongoing journey—a perpetual unfolding into deeper layers of unity. Each step reveals new dimensions of interconnectedness, new ways of experiencing the infinite within the finite. The seeker becomes the sought, the path becomes the destination, and the circle of existence completes itself.

As this chapter—and this journey—comes full circle, the essence of wholeness is distilled into a simple truth: there is no separation. All emanations, all beings, all experiences converge in the boundless field of existence. To return to the whole is to remember this truth, to live it, and to share it. It is the ultimate realization, the deepest mystery, and the most profound gift.

Epilogue

You have reached the end of this journey, but its echoes will continue to resonate within you. The words you've read, the concepts you've explored, and the connections you've made are not just memories of a reading; they are seeds planted in the fertile soil of your awareness.

Throughout these pages, you were invited to contemplate what lies beyond what the senses can perceive. More than stories and reflections, this book offered a glimpse into the subtle forces that shape existence—unseen yet ever-present. Now, it is up to you to integrate this knowledge into your everyday life.

The energies that connect all things do not end here. They flow through you, around you, among the people you meet, and the places you inhabit. Perhaps now you feel this more clearly. Perhaps you recognize that each moment carries a unique vibration, an invitation for you to actively participate in the universal dance.

Remember: understanding these forces is not an end in itself. It is a starting point for something greater. It is an invitation for you to become a channel of harmony, balance, and transformation in the world.

As you close this book, ask yourself: how can I apply the truths I have found here? How can I align more fully with the flows of energy that shape reality? And above all, how can I use this alignment to contribute to the well-being of all those connected with me in this vast web of life?

This is not the end of your journey. It is a new beginning, a new opportunity to hear the whispers of the universe and respond with intention and purpose. Carry with you the vibrations of this reading and allow them to resonate in all that you do. After all, the energies flowing within you are the same that sustain the cosmos.

With every thought, word, and action, you continue to write the story of these invisible forces—a story that is as much yours as it is of all that exists.

www.ingramcontent.com/pod-product-compliance
Lightning Source LLC
LaVergne TN
LVHW040052080526
838202LV00045B/3601